VEGAN INDIAN FOOD

RAGINI DEY

VEGAN INDIAN FOOD

RAGINI DEY

Hardie Grant
BOOKS

CONTENTS

	INTRODUCTION	6
	MY STORY	7
	A BRIEF HISTORY OF VEGANISM IN INDIA	10
	ADVICE ON SPICE	16
	BASIC RECIPES AND COOKING TECHNIQUES	24
	STARTERS AND SMALL BITES	32
	VEGETABLE DISHES	60

	PULSES	**96**
	RICE, BREAD AND POTATOES	**112**
	SALADS	**138**
	CHUTNEYS	**154**
	DESSERTS	**170**
	GLOSSARY	190
	INDEX	196
	ABOUT THE AUTHOR	202
	ACKNOWLEDGEMENTS	204

INTRODUCTION

If you are vegan, or would like to eat fewer animal products, Indian food is ideal. Vibrant, colourful and richly flavoured, it is described by some as God-like in its purity, yet devilishly sly as its spices lie in wait for unsuspecting palates. Indian cuisine has diversified throughout history; it is truly global, influencing and being influenced by all corners of the world. The vast array of vegan dishes is one of the most distinctive elements of Indian culture.

India has a long tradition of vegan and vegetarian food, beginning in ancient times and reflecting various influences – religious, cultural and countercultural – since then. Today, vegan food is becoming increasingly popular in the Western world for a number of reasons – not least, as a means of reducing our environmental footprint.

Is vegan Indian food difficult to cook? Not at all – it is just a matter of learning the rules before breaking them! The recipes presented here can all be prepared with ingredients you will find locally. I'm delighted to share them with you, and hope you will enjoy preparing them, whether it's one at a time for weeknight meals, or a few together for weekend feasts.

I was born Ragini Devika Mukerji in the tiny town of Mirzapur in North India, where my grandfather was the Civil Surgeon and in charge of the only hospital. It made perfect sense for his three daughters to trust the birth of their children to their dad. Mirzapur is famous for its brass and carpet industries and its vegetarian/vegan cuisine. Unfortunately, I never got to try any of its food, as soon after my birth, my mother and I were rushed away to join my father and his Bengali family in Calcutta.

Aged about 11, with my mother, father and brother in Delhi.

MY STORY

I was a chubby child who loved food. (In later life, my initials would come to stand for Rice Demolishing Machine.) Food in all its aspects played a huge role in my childhood. Contrary to the norms of the time, my father took a deep interest in overseeing the journey of a dish. Our menus were highly planned, with every recipe dissected in minute detail, from where the ingredients were grown, to the different techniques used in their cooking, to how the final dish should look and taste when it landed on our dining table. Together, we would do this for the next meal even before the previous one was eaten! The farmers and producers became my father's friends and one of the highlights of my childhood was a meal at a humble farm where we sat on the earth floor of a hut eating the simplest but most delicious of meals: freshly cooked okra (page 86) and puffed chapatti balloons (page 131). We were not vegetarian but, like millions of Indian families, our plates would be crowded with at least three vegetable preparations, a dal, a salad and a tiny quantity of fish or meat, all accompanied by steamed or pulao rice and bread.

When I was about six years old, we moved to Delhi. Different seasons, different vegetables, different spices, different ways of cooking! To avoid the intolerable summer heat, we fled to the Himalayas or the milder south during our annual holidays. A kaleidoscope of flavours, tastes and colours; a cacophony of smells; the cries from the street vendors' carts; the never-ending fields of red (chilli) and yellow (mustard); the taste of food served on freshly cut banana leaves glistening with the morning dew – these will be etched on my foodscape forever.

Around this time, my mother's parents retired to Dehradun in the Himalayan foothills. The house was surrounded by lychee, peach, plum and mango orchards, as well as vegetable gardens, and here my mother coined her favourite phrase: 'I am a vegetarian by choice.' For me, Dehradun was a paradise. We picked and ate fruit straight off the trees and also used it to make preserves, pickles and chutneys (page 154). One idyllic day followed another: being a help/hindrance in the veggie garden or kitchen, venturing too close to the woodfire brazier, and experimenting with my very first alfresco cooking experience in the shady canopy of the giant lychee tree. (Shared with cousins and friends all under the age of ten, the under-spiced and undercooked vegetable khichadi never tasted so good!)

Back in Delhi, I studied political science at university. Between the machinations of Machiavelli and Rousseau, I lived for the daily pick-me-up of the street-cart chickpea masala (page 103) with pillowy bhaturas (page 133). Despite these halcyon days, I came to realise that an academic career was not for me. Sitting an examination for the Institute of Hotel Management, Catering and Nutrition, Pusa, in New Delhi, I found myself one of thirteen girls (alongside 100 boys) to be accepted. Over the next three years, I learnt the art and science of transforming the humblest of ingredients into delicious, flavour-packed morsels. Next, I taught cookery at the Institute of Catering, Dadar, in Mumbai, where I was lucky enough to discover the secrets of western Indian cooking and its to-die-for street food.

When I landed in Adelaide in 1982, I found it beautiful, tranquil, quiet and welcoming. But sooner or later, I thought, I'm going to need some spice! The shops sold only the most basic of spices and even these were of doubtful quality. (If it weren't for my inherently law-abiding nature, I would have smuggled in the fabulous fragrances from my past.) People told me that they loved Indian food – especially the curried egg sandwich!

I took on various jobs. Cookery classes were popular and rewarding; a stint at Government House saw the Sunday roast become a Sunday curry; and during many years in aged care, I took the opportunity to cook some real food in place of the residents' usual premixes and tins.

Seven years later, I opened the Spice Kitchen, a humble takeaway in the cosmopolitan suburb of Kensington, in an attempt to share the real cooking of regional India in all its diversity and majesty. We held cooking classes, I produced some cooking manuals, and we manufactured our own range of natural, authentic spice blends that were vegan and gluten-free (two terms rarely used at the time). Gradually, the Spice Kitchen grew into a critically acclaimed, multi-awarded restaurant, allowing me to showcase my food on television and write a 'proper' book.

After twenty-six years of rewarding but exhausting work, I sold the restaurant in 2015, planning to downsize. When my dream to run a one-woman kitchen was thwarted by Covid, I became involved with the Adelaide Farmers' Market. As I got to know the producers, I gained a new respect for the work they put in to produce the most delicious fruit and vegetables, and an understanding of the importance of seasonality. I remain in awe of the variety and diversity of these lovingly grown products – such as Buddha's hand and purple cauliflower – and of how wonderful they taste.

One can never be bored when cooking with vegetables, fruits, grains and pulses. From the simplest salad or dal to the most complex dish, vegetables lend themselves to many different cooking techniques, from stovetop to fermenting, preserving and smoking. Spices, of course, are the jewel in the crown and my go-to ingredient in vegan cooking.

My food philosophy emphasises eating and cooking ...

- with curiosity
- with generosity and love
- without harm to oneself or anything else
- with enjoyment for friends and family
- with natural, unprocessed ingredients as far as possible.

In general, I'm not a fan of plant-based meat substitutes. These plants are delicious in their own right – why mess around with them to obtain an inferior product?

It is my greatest pleasure to be able to share a few of my favourite vegan recipes with you. These are little gems that you will find yourself cooking again and again. This book is not meant to be a comprehensive tome, but rather, an easy and delicious entree to the inexhaustible world of Indian vegan cooking.

RAGINI DEY

The culinary history of India goes back thousands of years. In ancient times, meat was consumed by the Brahmins (the highest of the four Hindu castes, from which priests were traditionally drawn) and the kings. However, from the fourth century BCE, vegetarianism began to appear in particular religious sects. (In India, the terms 'vegan' and 'vegetarian' are often used interchangeably.) The earliest records of vegetarianism are from Indian images and writings from the Indus Valley – one of the oldest civilisations in the world – in 3300 BCE. Archaeologists even discovered evidence of natural dies used to extrude pasta.

A BRIEF HISTORY OF VEGANISM IN INDIA

In the ninth century BCE, Parsvanatha founded the Jain religion, which is often considered the strictest form of vegetarianism. According to the writings of Chinese pilgrims who visited the region, the killing of animals, the consumption of alcohol and the eating of vegetables that grew underground (such as onions and garlic) were strictly forbidden. Even green leafy vegetables were not to be eaten, in case any worms were ingested by mistake. In the sixth century, under Mahavira (regarded as the founder of Jainism in its current form), Jainism was further cemented in India. Its central doctrine is that all nature is alive and that every living thing, including rocks and plants, has a soul. Jains believe that to protect one's own soul, one must treat all other souls with non-violence (*ahimsa* in Sanskrit). Gautam Buddha (563–483 BCE), a Nepalese prince who left home in search of Nirvana and founded Buddhism, also preached vegetarianism but in a more moderate way.

Jainism and Buddhism both had a major influence on one of India's greatest emperors. Ashoka (304–232 BCE) inscribed his moral code – or dharma – on sandstone pillars and rocks all over his kingdom, which stretched across the entire Indian subcontinent. Under his rule, vegetarianism gained popularity throughout society, including among the Brahmins. Almost two thousand years later, in the sixteenth century, the Mogul ruler Akbar was so influenced by the teachings of Ashoka that he became largely vegetarian, further strengthening the tradition. Vegetarianism became linked with ideas of hierarchy and social status.

Indian vegetarianism also influenced the ancient Greeks, who admired the ascetic lifestyle of the nut-eating, water-drinking Indian. In the Middle Ages, such famous explorers as Marco Polo, and scientists such as Leonardo da Vinci, extolled the virtues of the honest, regularly bathed, spiritual, healthy and long-living vegetarian Indians.

European intellectuals, including Jean-Jacques Rousseau and Jacques-Henri Bernardin de Saint-Pierre, credited the Indian vegetarian diet with the continent's superior skills in the arts, sciences, laws and games. Voltaire praised the Brahmins as enlightened advocates of a natural diet, telling a story where the hero eats a meal of a thousand delicious dishes with no meat. British literary luminaries Percy Shelley and George Bernard Shaw, who were both familiar with India, also supported a vegetarian lifestyle.

Back in India, the Theosophical Society, which began in New York but shifted its headquarters to Chennai (formerly known as Madras) in the late 1870s, was calling for Indian independence from Britain. Mahatma Gandhi, who had grown up in the Hindu- and Jain-dominated state of Gujarat, was attracted by the teachings of the society, which promoted vegetarianism on health and ecological, as well as spiritual, grounds. Gandhi, who became known as the 'father of India' as a result of his independence movement, was heavily influenced by Jain and Hindu principles of non-violence in both his diet and his politics. Hindu principles of compassion and empathy continue to resonate with many vegans today.

In the 1960s, India garnered western interest, largely through the hippie counterculture that began in the United States and spread to many parts of the world. Even the Beatles studied transcendental meditation in India and all four members of the band were vegetarian at some point in their lives. At the same time, Indians engaged in their own experiments. Women who previously would not even have accepted a cup of tea at a non-vegetarian home started cooking meat for their husbands and children. And others who would not cook meat at home tried non-vegetarian dishes in restaurants. On the other hand, many meat eaters declared at least two days in the week meat-free.

Today, in a chaotic world where people are struggling to make sense of things, many Indians are rediscovering their spiritual roots and finding that veganism can provide some answers. In a kind of reversal, veganism's popularity in the west – as a response to climate change in particular – is attracting a whole new following in India. Traditional eating places – some that were started hundreds of years ago by temple cooks – are drawing a new clientele. Newly branded 'vegan' restaurants are all the rage, popularised by influencers and trendsetting Bollywood actors. India's vibrant street-food culture has a special role to play in the popularity of economical vegetarian and vegan food, which exists not only for the 'foodie' but for the common person, who may have no other way to fill their stomach. Flavoured with natural spices, these dishes are never bland. Rather than substituting vegetables for meat, each recipe is created around a particular vegan ingredient. The flamboyant Mukesh Ambani, India's wealthiest entrepreneur, flags a humble vegan restaurant as his favourite place to eat.

Today, many Indians have chosen not to eat meat in line with concerns about the treatment of animals or unhygienic conditions of production. Medical research pointing towards a connection between increased meat consumption and life-threatening diseases has also played a part in convincing Indians to revert to veganism. In a country with such a rich history and diversity of delicious vegan recipes that are distinct to its many regions, where spiritual practice, politics and food go hand in hand, where the cow has been venerated as holy from time immemorial, and where the ancient scriptures set out best-practice guidelines for achieving optimum health, this should not be a matter of surprise – but one for celebration.

An Indian kitchen is a fragrant kitchen. The aroma of spices permeates every part of the body and soul, nourishing and satisfying the palate. Spices and herbs are the foundation blocks of Indian cuisine, and are certainly not restricted to traditional curries. As with all good recipes, balance is the key. Used individually, or in harmonious blends, spices bring perfection to any number of Indian dishes. On the other hand, there is nothing as terrible as a clumsily spiced dish. The careful blending of different spice quantities is required to successfully achieve those few master dishes that use up to thirty-six spices.

Where at all possible, begin with whole spices – seeds, fruit or bark. They have much more flavour than powdered varieties. Dry-roast or heat whole spices before grinding using a mortar and pestle or electric spice grinder to release their maximum flavour and taste. Stay away from mass-produced, premixed curry powders and pastes; apart from everything tasting the same, you will never be able to duplicate the freshness and intensity achieved with freshly blended spices, where subtlety shines through alongside bolder, more vibrant tastes. A grey turmeric or cardamom will produce a grey result. Always buy in small quantities and store in dark, dry places.

Don't be afraid to try unfamiliar spices to get to know their distinctive flavours. For vegetables or delicately flavoured ingredients, use only one or two spices to bring out the taste – such as onion seeds and chilli with cauliflower. Experiment with different combinations – your imagination and tastebuds will do the rest.

ADVICE ON SPICE

ESSENTIAL SPICES

AJWAIN SEEDS
These tiny grey seeds come from the same family as cumin and parsley. In taste, they are similar to celery seeds with overtones of thyme. In vegan Indian cooking, they are used to flavour deep-fried foods and vegetables. Try ajwain seeds stir-fried with garlic, eggplant, tomatoes, coriander (cilantro) leaves and chilli.

ALLSPICE
This berry comes from the *Pimenta dioica*, a small tree native to the West Indies. The fruit is gathered when green and unripe and dried in the sun, where the berries turn black. Allspice has the flavour of cloves, cinnamon and nutmeg. It is also known as Jamaica pepper, and in India as *kababchini*.

AMCHUR
Green mangoes are dried and ground to obtain this sour tangy spice, used to lift the taste of popular snacks, such as samosas and pakoras. Amchur is especially useful if you want to achieve a sour taste like lemon or tamarind without the liquid content.

ASAFOETIDA
A very sharp-tasting spice derived from a resinous gum of the fennel family, asafoetida is used sparingly in vegetarian dishes and with lentils. North Indian recipes, especially from Kashmir, include asafoetida but always in very minute amounts. The gum is said to aid digestion and gives a unique taste, which you may either love or hate. Its aroma after cooking has been compared with that of truffles. For a simple recipe, add a tiny amount to hot vegan ghee with julienned ginger and fresh green peas.

CARDAMOM
Also known as the Queen of Spices, cardamom is the fruit of a reed-like plant from the mountains near the Malabar Coast in India. Two types are commonly used in Indian cooking: the small and more delicate green cardamom pods with thin black seeds inside, and the large brown cardamom pods, which are at least four times the size of the green. The pods release a beautiful fragrance when crushed and the seeds have a strong, sweetish flavour. Cardamom is an essential ingredient of garam masala (page 20), and is often used to flavour sweet dishes, such as custards, ice creams and rice puddings.

CHILLIES
In Indian cooking, chillies are generally fresh green (unripe), dried red or ground as red chilli powder. The three cannot be interchanged in recipes as they all have different flavours. Fresh chillies also vary in pungency. A good guide is often the size: the smaller the chilli, the hotter it is. You can reduce the heat of chillies by removing their seeds and the attached membrane before cooking. Alternatively, if you prefer more heat, add some freshly chopped chilli to your dish after cooking.

CINNAMON
Cinnamon is the bark of an evergreen tree belonging to the laurel family, native to Sri Lanka, the Indian subcontinent, Malaysia and Indonesia. The outer bark is stripped away, and the inner bark is loosened and dried. Often confused with cassia bark, true cinnamon is softer and has a more subtle aroma. Cinnamon leaves are used to flavour curries, stocks and rice.

CLOVES

One of the oldest-known spices, cloves were regularly used by the Ancient Egyptians and the Romans. The clove (myrtle) tree can grow to six metres and its unopened flower buds are carefully harvested. Known for its preservation qualities, cloves are used in both savoury and sweet Indian dishes.

CORIANDER

The small round or oval brown seeds of the coriander plant are one of the most popularly used spices in Indian cooking. The seeds are usually roasted and ground before use. Fresh coriander (cilantro) leaves are used for flavouring curries, salads, chutneys and as a garnish.

CUMIN

Used either whole or as a powder, cumin is widely grown in Europe, India and Mexico. Cumin is said to stimulate the appetite and aid digestion. It is frequently used in curries, biscuits, couscous and fried rice. Fry whole cumin seeds in vegan ghee and add to cooked vegetables, lentils and rice.

FENNEL SEEDS

The dried fruit of a perennial herb of the parsley family, fennel is grown in Europe, India, the Middle East and Argentina. The seed resembles cumin in shape but is green and slightly fatter with a licorice-like flavour. Fennel is used whole and ground in breads, pickles and sauces. It is also an ingredient of the Indian five-spice mix panch phoron (page 21). Cook rice with fennel seeds for a really aromatic dish.

FENUGREEK

These squarish, yellowish-brown seeds have a slightly bitter flavour. They are used either whole or ground to flavour vegetables and curries. The leaves are used as a vegetable, and dried fenugreek is essential for certain recipes. Add a few seeds to soup stocks or, with curry leaves, to vegetable soups for that special South Indian taste.

MUSTARD

An ancient spice grown in most parts of the world, mustard seeds are used in both Western and Indian recipes. The pungency of the seeds is fully released when they are ground and mixed with water. In India, both the yellow and black seeds are used in cooking.

Mustard oil, made from ground mustard seeds, is used widely in East and North India. Mustard seeds and mustard oil are used frequently in vegetable dishes and when pickling fruits.

NUTMEG AND MACE

These two spices are from the same fruit grown in Malaysia, the Indian subcontinent, Indonesia and the West Indies. Nutmeg is the seed, protected by a thin shell. The shell has a coat of orange flesh which, when dried, becomes mace. Although the aroma of mace is similar to that of nutmeg, mace is sweeter. Nutmeg is used finely grated in sweets, curries and sauces, while mace is coarsely crushed and used to flavour soups and stocks, as well as sweet dishes and rich Mughal curries and biryanis. When buying nutmeg, choose seeds that are round, compact, have an oily appearance and feel heavy for their size.

ONION SEEDS

Sometimes known as black cumin, these tiny black seeds have a sweet flavour. An ingredient of the Indian five-spice mix panch phoron (page 21), onion seeds are also used as a pickling spice and to flavour breads.

PEPPER

The seeds or berries of the plant *Piper nigrum*, native to the Malabar Coast of India, are dried to make both black pepper (the whole berry) and white pepper (husk removed). Pepper is used whole, crushed coarsely or finely ground, and is also an ingredient of garam masala (page 20).

POPPY SEEDS

In India, white poppy seeds are mainly used for their nutty flavour and thickening quality when added to rich curries, such as kormas and vegetables dishes. They are usually soaked in hot water for at least two hours, then ground to a paste. Add to cooked potatoes for a delicious vegetable accompaniment.

SAFFRON

The world's most expensive spice is made from the dried stamens of a type of crocus that grows in the Mediterranean, the Middle East and India. A quarter of a million plants are required to yield 450 g (1 lb) of saffron. Buy only from reliable sources, as fake saffron is often sold as a cheaper substitute. Saffron has an ethereal fragrance with a pale yellow colour and should be infused in warm milk to obtain the best results. Use in stocks, soups, rice and desserts.

TURMERIC

A ginger-like rhizome grown in India and the West Indies. In India it is usually dried whole and ground to a powder. The hard resinous flesh of the dried root varies from a dark orange to a deep reddish-brown. In its powder form it is usually bright yellow. Turmeric is not only used for its colour and flavour but also as a preservative.

ROASTING AND GRINDING WHOLE SPICES

Some recipes call for spices that are already ground. These recipes tend to require a subtler mix of flavours. Some recipes call for whole spices that then have to be ground freshly – the result is a greater freshness and a greater intensity of flavour. Then there are recipes that require whole spices to be roasted and ground. This is the process of dry-roasting, or dry-toasting, whole spices before grinding them. This intensifies the colour, flavour and aroma of the spices, and brings a greater richness and depth to the taste of the finished dish. Using spices that are already ground will save a bit of time, but they will not give the same result.

To dry-roast whole spices, heat a small frying pan over a medium heat. Add all the whole spices that the recipe requires to the pan and heat them gently, stirring continuously, until they are warmed through and have started to release their aroma. This should take about 2–5 minutes, depending on the quantity and type of spices you are working with. Take care not to overheat the spices, as this will destroy their colour and flavour. If the spices are too hot to touch, they have been burnt.

Remove the spices from the heat and leave to cool, then grind in an electric grinder or use a mortar and pestle to get the desired coarseness or fineness.

SPICE MIXES

The word 'masala' is a generic term that refers to a combination, or mix, of spices. The following spice mixes are commonly used blends.

GARAM MASALA
Makes 3 tablespoons

Garam masala has a very delicate flavour, so it's best to make it fresh every time you need it. The word garam means 'warm' and refers to the heating properties of the spices used in this blend. According to Ayurvedic medicine – a Hindu system of traditional medicine that originated in India – all spices are considered to be either heating or cooling, and you maintain an equilibrium of heating and cooling elements in the body by watching what you eat.

Garam masala is sometimes sprinkled on vegan dishes right at the end of cooking.

3 teaspoons cumin seeds
1 teaspoon green cardamom pods
1 teaspoon black peppercorns
5 cm (2 in) cinnamon stick
1 teaspoon cloves

Heat a small frying pan over a medium heat. Add the spices and heat them gently, stirring continuously, for about 2 minutes, or until they release their aroma. Cool, then transfer to an electric grinder or use a mortar and pestle and process to a fine powder. Use as directed in the recipe. Alternatively, you can store in an airtight container in the cupboard for 2 days, or in the refrigerator or freezer for a week, although it will lose some of its subtle aroma.

CHAAT MASALA
Makes 6 tablespoons

This is a piquant, tangy, sweet–spicy blend that is sprinkled on salads, starters and sliced or diced fruit – fruit chaat is a popular snack bought from street vendors in India. This particular spice blend stores well, so it can be made in advance or in larger quantities.

1 tablespoon cumin seeds
1 tablespoon black peppercorns
½ teaspoon cloves
½ tablespoon dried mint leaves
¼ teaspoon ajwain seeds
¼ teaspoon asafoetida
1 tablespoon rock salt
1 teaspoon ground amchur
1 teaspoon ground ginger
1 teaspoon chilli powder

Heat a small frying pan over a medium heat. Add the cumin, peppercorns, cloves, dried mint, ajwain seeds and asafoetida and heat gently, stirring continuously, for about 1 minute, or until they release their aroma. Cool, then transfer to an electric grinder or a mortar and pestle. Add the salt, amchur, ginger and chilli and process to a fine powder. Use as directed in the recipe, or store in an airtight container in the cupboard for up to 3 months.

BALTI MASALA
Makes 5 tablespoons

This spice mix gets its name from the cast-iron bucket, known as a balti, that was originally used to cook balti-style dishes. The karahi (a small Indian wok) has now replaced the bucket! Add to vegan dishes while stir-frying over a high heat for the distinctive bold taste of balti cooking.

- 1 teaspoon chilli flakes
- 2 tablespoons coriander seeds
- 1 teaspoon black peppercorns
- 2.5 cm (1 in) cinnamon stick
- ½ teaspoon cloves
- ½ teaspoon green cardamom pods
- 1 teaspoon dried fenugreek leaves

Put all the spices in an electric grinder or use a mortar and pestle and process until coarsely crushed or ground. Use as directed in the recipe, or store in an airtight container in the cupboard for up to 1 month.

PANCH PHORON
Makes 2 tablespoons

Here is a spice mix from Bengal that uses whole spices rather than spices that have been crushed or ground. It is added early in the cooking process. The contrasting and complementary flavours of the spices – pungent, bitter, sweet, astringent – bounce off each other to provide a special taste.

- 1 teaspoon black mustard seeds
- 1 teaspoon yellow mustard seeds
- 1 teaspoon fenugreek seeds
- 1 teaspoon fennel seeds
- 1 teaspoon nigella (kalonji)

Toss the whole spices together in a small bowl. Use as directed in the recipe, or store in an airtight container in the cupboard for up to 1 year.

SAFFRON INFUSION
Makes 2 tablespoons

Using an infusion of saffron threads in milk distributes the saffron flavour more evenly and strongly during cooking than simply adding the saffron threads to the pan. The infusion must be made fresh, so reduce the amount you make if the recipe requires less.

- 3 saffron threads
- 2 tablespoons milk

Gently heat the saffron and milk in a small saucepan over a low heat for 2 minutes. Remove from the heat and leave to stand for 20 minutes to let the flavour develop and intensify. Use as directed in the recipe.

Indian cooking involves some basic recipes and techniques that you'll use again and again. There are page references to these basics throughout the book. You'll find them quite simple, and they are worth learning because they will make a difference to the taste and texture of the dishes you cook. With them, your food will have that magical authentic Indian flavour.

BASIC RECIPES AND COOKING TECHNIQUES

BASIC RECIPES

GINGER PASTE
Makes 250 g (9 oz/1 cup)

Indian dishes are never thickened with wheat flour – a real boon for those who are gluten-intolerant. Instead, sauces are thickened with other ingredients, which also add flavour. One of these is ginger paste, which gives body and a different taste from that obtained with grated ginger. It is important to use the preparation method stipulated in the recipe, as different methods give different results. Also, it is always better to make your own paste, as store-bought pastes often contain preservatives and additives that distort the flavour.

100 g (3½ oz) fresh ginger

Peel and chop the ginger. Process in a food processor with 125 ml (4 fl oz/½ cup) water to form a smooth paste. Use as directed in the recipe, or store in an airtight container in the refrigerator for up to 2 weeks.

GARLIC PASTE
Makes 250 g (9 oz/1 cup)

Along with ginger paste, garlic paste is commonly used to thicken sauces. It results in a smoother texture and subtler flavour than chopped or crushed garlic, which gives a different, fresher taste and more coarsely textured sauce.

100 g (3½ oz) garlic cloves

Peel and chop the garlic. Process in a food processor with 125 ml (4 fl oz/½ cup) water to form a smooth paste. Use as directed in the recipe, or store in an airtight container in the refrigerator for up to 2 weeks.

TAMARIND PULP
Makes 250 ml (8½ fl oz/1 cup)

Tamarind is a popular souring agent used in Indian cooking. In North India, it is usually combined with something sweet, such as jaggery (dark brown unrefined sugar), molasses or sugar, to provide a sweet and sour flavour in dishes. In the west and south it is normally used in vegetable preparations to add an intensely sour flavour. Tamarind is available in dried seedless form, as a concentrate or already pulped in refrigerated tubs. I prefer the dried tamarind that can be reconstituted into a pulp (as described here) when required, rather than the concentrate, which has an overly strong colour and flavour, or the ready-made pulp, which is perishable.

100 g (3½ oz) dried tamarind

Heat the dried tamarind and 250 ml (8½ fl oz/1 cup) water in a small saucepan over a medium heat, stirring occasionally, for about 3–5 minutes, or until the tamarind is softened and disintegrating. Strain through a mesh strainer into a bowl to obtain a smooth pulp. It will keep in an airtight container in the refrigerator for up to 2 weeks.

FRESH COCONUT MILK
Makes 250 ml (8½ fl oz/1 cup)

Fresh coconut milk has a sweet flavour all its own. It also tends not to be oily. Although making fresh coconut milk is not as convenient as opening a tin, the recipes in this book will be vastly improved with the use of fresh milk. (However, if you don't have access to fresh coconut, the recipes will also work with tinned coconut milk.)

To make fresh milk, you will need freshly grated coconut, which is available from Indian grocery stores. (Make sure it is not frozen, as this tends to lessen the flavour.) If freshly grated is not available and you need to grate your own, cut the white coconut flesh into large pieces and grate with a grater. Alternatively, use a food processor fitted with the grater attachment to process, or simply process with the blade attachment to chop finely.

100 g (3½ oz/2 cups) freshly grated coconut

Put the grated coconut in a large bowl, pour in 375 ml (12½ fl oz/1½ cups) hot water and steep for about 30 minutes. Line a mesh strainer with a clean square of muslin (cheesecloth) and strain the liquid through the muslin into a bowl underneath. Press down firmly on the grated coconut in the muslin-lined strainer to extract all the thick rich liquid from it. Use the coconut milk as directed, or store in an airtight container in the refrigerator for up to 3 days.

NOTE: Do not discard the grated coconut. Instead, use it to thicken curries, although be aware that it will not have a strong taste. Or you can use it to repeat the process of making fresh coconut milk up to three times. You will obtain first-, second- and third-strength coconut milk that can be added to recipes for strong or light flavour and richness.

STEAMED OR BOILED RICE
Serves 4

Steamed rice, especially steamed basmati rice, is the best complement for most curries. It is the everyday rice eaten in most Indian homes. North Indians prefer bread or biryanis and fried rice preparations. But while steamed rice is popular throughout India, it is deemed an insult to offer it to guests or serve it on festive occasions – it shows that the host did not take the trouble to serve something more elaborate.

200 g (7 oz/1 cup) basmati rice or other long-grain rice, washed and drained

To steam the rice, put it in a shallow heavy-based saucepan. Pour in 375 ml (12½ fl oz/1½ cups) water, stir and bring to a boil over a medium heat. Reduce the heat to low, cover and cook for about 20 minutes. Do not uncover or stir during the cooking time; this ensures that the rice cooks evenly and does not break up. Remove from the heat and, still covered, leave to rest for 10 minutes before serving. (This allows the rice grains to plump up to their maximum length.)

The rice can also be cooked by the boiling method. Put the rice and 1 litre (34 fl oz/4 cups) water in a large saucepan. Bring to a boil over a high heat, then reduce the heat to medium and cook, uncovered, for about 20 minutes, or until the rice is soft. Drain in a sieve but do not rinse in cold water.

The best steamed or boiled rice should be firm to the touch and al dente, not mushy.

COOKING TECHNIQUES

DEEP-FRYING

In India, a karahi (Indian wok) is used for deep-frying, but a Chinese wok is a good alternative. The wok shape means that less oil is needed, compared with a saucepan. However, the rounded bottom of these woks is only safe to use on a gas stovetop. Special woks are available to use on induction stovetops and are very efficient. If you don't have a suitable wok, you can use an electric deep-fryer.

Use any oil without a pronounced flavour, but that has a high smoke point, so that the oil can be heated to high temperatures without burning, spitting or giving off noxious fumes, and the food won't take on the particular flavour of the oil.

Different foods are deep-fried at different temperatures – the temperature of the oil can range from 160°C (320°F) to 210°C (410°F), depending on the item being cooked. For example, a samosa is deep-fried in oil heated to a medium heat (180°C/350°F) so the pastry cooks while the filling inside is only heated through. On the other hand, a crumbed vegetable patty needs the oil to be at a high heat (200°C/400°F) to cook all the way through. Breads such as pooris also need oil at a high heat (200–210°C/400–410°F) to make them puff out, and are fried for a very short time only – about 40–60 seconds. A thicker bread, such as a bhatura, needs slightly less heat (190–200°C/375–400°F) and is fried for longer – about 2 minutes – as it needs extra time to cook.

You can check that the oil has reached the correct temperature with a kitchen thermometer. Alternatively, drop 1 teaspoon of pastry, dough or batter in the oil. If it rises immediately to the surface, the oil is ready. If it settles at the bottom, the oil is not hot enough and the cooked food will be greasy. If the batter turns black, it is very hot and suitable for deep-frying breads but would burn very small items.

Avoid the temptation to fry too many items at once as this lowers the temperature of the oil and makes the food greasy. To avoid being splashed with hot oil, don't drop the items to be cooked in from a height. Instead, always put them on a slotted spoon or frying spoon, position the spoon as close as possible to the hot oil (being careful not to burn yourself) and let them slide in gently.

PRESSURE COOKING

The modern pressure cooker is a boon to Indian cooking. While instructions for its use haven't been included in the recipe methods in this book, it can reduce the cooking time of certain dishes by about 75 per cent.

You can use a pressure cooker to make the cooking of lentils, dried beans and chickpeas a quick and easy task. After any necessary soaking and rinsing, put the lentils, beans or chickpeas in the pressure cooker with the specified amount of water and cook for one-quarter of the time specified in the recipe, or until they are the required softness.

THE DHUNGAR METHOD

This method is a traditional way to add a fabulous, smoky flavour to dishes such as curries, dals and mashed vegetables after they are cooked.

Prepare the ingredients you want to smoke in a large, heatproof bowl. Using tongs, heat a small piece of charcoal on a naked gas flame or a barbecue. Once the charcoal is glowing red-hot, carefully place it in a small metal container. Sprinkle the hot charcoal with about a teaspoon of any spice of your choice, then immediately pour 1 tablespoon of vegan ghee or oil on top; this will generate a lot of smoke. Quickly place the charcoal container in the heatproof bowl, cover the bowl with aluminium foil or a tight-fitting lid and leave for about 20 minutes before uncovering and proceeding with the next step in the recipe.

VEGAN SUBSTITUTES

There are many alternatives to non-vegan ingredients – and more are becoming available all the time. The recipes in this book call for the following vegan ingredients, which are readily available.

VEGAN BUTTER
Typically made from oil (coconut, canola, etc.) and vegan milk (oat, cauliflower, soy, etc.), and available to buy, but also easy to make at home.

VEGAN CONDENSED MILK
Typically made from oats, rice or coconut milk, and sweetened.

VEGAN CREAM
Available from soy, oat, rice, almond and coconut bases.

VEGAN GHEE
A substitute for ghee, which is one of the primary fats used in Indian vegetarian cooking. There are many choices available using base ingredients such as coconut or macadamia nuts, and flavoured with aromatic leaves such as guava. You can make your own by melting vegan butter and decanting the clear fat.

VEGAN MILK
Made from a variety of beans, nuts, seeds and grains; the most popular are soy, oat and almond milks.

VEGAN MILK POWDERS
Coconut, soy and oat milk powders are widely available.

A NOTE ON TIMES, MEASUREMENTS, PANS AND TASTING

The preparation and cooking time I have given for each recipe is approximate, as many factors influence the actual time taken. It is likely to take you a little longer the first time that you prepare a recipe, but you will get faster as you gain confidence in the methodology.

Factors such as the pans used and the heat of the cooktop have a bearing on the cooking time. For wet curries (such as Vegetable moilee, page 92), I recommend using wide, heavy-based saucepans so that you have plenty of room to stir and the ingredients are not jammed together. Cover the saucepan with a lid when recommended as this speeds up the process. Also, refrain from checking on your dish too often as this allows the steam to escape, increasing the cooking time.

For dryer recipes (such as Pumpkin with panch phoron, page 73), use a small wok or, ideally, a karahi (a traditional round-based pan that is slightly deeper than an Asian wok and made of a thicker metal, such as cast iron – available in bigger Indian stores). Otherwise, a deeper frying pan is suitable. Just make sure you have a well-fitting lid; this allows the vegetables to cook in their own juices without the need to add much water or stock, leading to a more concentrated flavour.

Other recipe books or chefs may encourage constant tasting as you go along. However, with Indian food, the whole flavour profile changes as the dish cooks, along with its texture, consistency and flavour. So, I recommend tasting only near the end of cooking, to adjust seasoning.

This book uses 15 ml (½ fl oz) tablespoons; cooks using 20 ml (¾ fl oz) tablespoons should be scant with their tablespoon measurements. Metric cup measurements are used (i.e. 250 ml for 1 cup); in the US, a cup is slightly smaller (8 fl oz), so American cooks should be generous with their cup measurements. Additionally, the recipes were cooked in a fan-forced or convection oven; if using a conventional oven, increase the temperature by 35°C (95°F). Finally, all instances of sugar refer to granulated cane sugar unless otherwise specified.

Happy cooking!

BASIC RECIPES AND COOKING TECHNIQUES

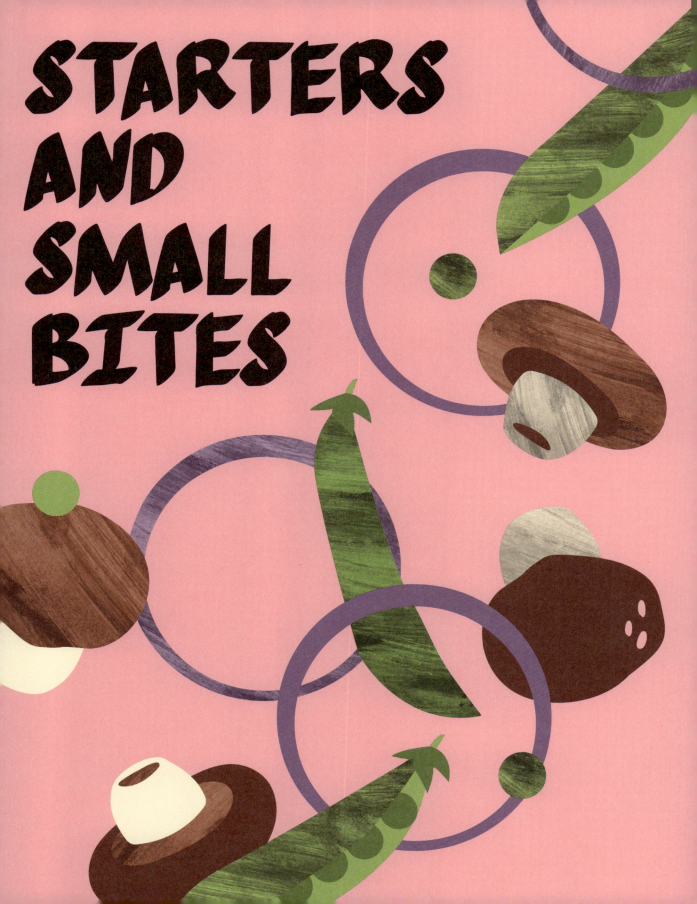

Masala pappadams चटपटे पापर	36
Pakoras पकौडे	38
Vegetable samosas सब्जी समोसे	41
Mulligatawny soup दाल और सब्जी का मुलगि शोरबा	42
Mushroom and coconut shorba ढींगरी और नारियल का शोरबा	43
Pao bhajee पाओ भाजी	44
Onion uthappams प्याज उत्तपम	46
Cabbage bondas पत्तागोभी बोंडा	49
Dahi ke kababs दही के कबाब	50
Banana chilli and potato pakoras मर्रिच और आलू के पकौडे	51
Grilled swiss brown mushrooms with spiced breadcrumbs and green peas ढींगरी भरवां, मटर और डबल रोटी चूर	53
Beetroot and vegetable 'chops' चुकंदर चॉप	55
Upma उपमा	56
Masoor dal wadas मसूर दाल वडा	57
Onion bhajees प्याज भाजी	59

In India, people love to snack throughout the day. Morning tea, brunch, light lunch and afternoon tea all provide an opportunity to bite into a samosa, break off a piece of bread and dip it in dal, salivate over a grilled vegetable kabab or enjoy the fresh crispness of a pakora. The recipes in this chapter come from all over India, and while the ingredients can change from region to region, the result is the same – deliciously fresh and tasty dishes that satisfy the momentary appetite for something small.

Most Indian families do not eat a formal course-by-course meal, and starters and small dishes are often incorporated into banquet-style meals. Perhaps start off with Masala pappadums (page 36) and a couple of chutneys for dipping (page 154), before moving on to traditional Pakoras (page 38) and Dahi ke kababs (page 50), served alongside larger vegetable dishes. Recipes such as Vegetable samosas (page 41) and Masoor dal wadas (page 57) work equally well served with pre-dinner drinks or as finger foods at a party, or even as a late-night snack after a night out. Alternatively, try Grilled Swiss brown mushrooms with spiced breadcrumbs and green peas (page 53) for a breakfast with a twist, or indulge in the great combination of toasted buttery bread and vegetable dip, Pao bhajee (page 44).

Many of the recipes in this chapter can be prepared ahead of time, which means you don't need to be in the kitchen when everyone else is enjoying them. So, sit back, relax and indulge in the tastiest small treats India has to offer.

STARTERS AND SMALL BITES

PREPARATION TIME
5 minutes

COOKING TIME
10 minutes

SERVES
4 (makes 8)

---

250 ml (8½ fl oz/1 cup) vegetable or sunflower oil for shallow-frying

8 plain pappadums

2 tablespoons chopped coriander (cilantro) leaves

pinch of chilli powder

2 tablespoons chaat masala (page 20)

2 tablespoons shredded (grated dried) coconut

This recipe takes the ubiquitous pappadum to the next level! The word pappadum comes from the Sanskrit *parpata*, meaning a kind of thin, crisp cake baked or fried in oil. Pappadums can be served with drinks or as an appetiser. In South India they are normally served with the main meal, crumbled and mixed with rice and curries to provide an exciting crunch. They can be made of lentils, sago, rice or potato. They are usually fried, although some brands can be cooked on a hotplate or under the grill (broiler).

चटपटे पापर

MASALA PAPPADUMS

Heat the oil in a wok or frying pan over a high heat until it is smoking. Cook 1 pappadum at a time for about 2–3 seconds, or until crisp. Remove from the frying pan immediately and place on a large tray. Repeat the process for the remaining pappadums.

Sprinkle the pappadums with the coriander, chilli powder, chaat masala and coconut. Serve immediately.

NOTE: You can also deep-fry the pappadums if you prefer. Heat 500 ml (17 fl oz/ 2 cups) oil in a wok or deep-fryer to 200°C (400°F; see page 27), then continue as for the method above.

Quick to make and quick to eat, these crispy fried fritters are a popular finger food in India.

This recipe is for the traditional pakora – the tempura-style individual piece of vegetable fried in batter. There are many types of pakoras, including bread pakoras (essentially bread sandwiched with a green chutney and dipped into the pakora batter). They are a really versatile snack to make when friends drop in unannounced, as you are sure to have at least one or two vegetables that you can use to dip in the batter. Pakoras are delicious served with Tamarind and ginger chutney (page 160) or Green chutney (page 161).

पकोड़े
PAKORAS

To make the batter, mix together the besan, ajwain seeds, chilli powder, vinegar and salt in a medium bowl, then make a well in the centre. Gradually pour in 275 ml (9½ fl oz) water while whisking together the ingredients to form a batter that has a coating consistency – it should coat the back of the spoon and gently drip down. Stir in a little more water, if necessary, to achieve the right consistency.

Heat the oil in a wok or deep-fryer to 180°C (350°F; see page 27). Dip the individual pieces of vegetable in the batter and deep-fry a few at a time until golden brown and cooked through – about 2–3 minutes for the spinach leaves, 4 minutes for the eggplant batons and onion rings, and 5 minutes for the potato rounds and cauliflower florets. Remove from the oil and drain on kitchen towels. Serve hot.

PREPARATION TIME
15 minutes

COOKING TIME
12 minutes

SERVES
4 (makes 12–16)

---

vegetable or sunflower oil for deep-frying

250 g (9 oz) prepared mixed vegetables, choosing from the following:
- 200 g (7 oz) English spinach, stems discarded, individual leaves separated
- 1 small eggplant (aubergine), sliced into 2.5 cm (1 in) thick batons
- 1 large onion, sliced into thick rings
- 1 large potato, peeled and sliced into 5 mm (¼ in) rounds
- 4 cauliflower florets, broken into small florets about 2.5 cm (1 in) across

BATTER

110 g (4 oz/1 cup) besan (chickpea flour)

1 teaspoon ajwain seeds

1 teaspoon chilli powder

2 teaspoons white vinegar

½–1 teaspoon salt, or to taste

PREPARATION TIME
40 minutes

COOKING TIME
15 minutes

SERVES
4

---

2 sheets ready-made vegan shortcrust (pie) pastry (see Note)

vegetable or sunflower oil for deep-frying

FILLING

150 g (5½ oz/1 cup) diced mixed vegetables, choosing 4 of the following:
- 1 small potato, peeled
- 1 small carrot, peeled
- 50 g (1¾ oz/¼ cup) corn kernels cut from the cob
- ½ small sweet potato, peeled
- 6 green beans, trimmed
- 40 g (1½ oz/¼ cup) shelled fresh or frozen peas
- 2 cauliflower florets

1 tablespoon vegetable or sunflower oil

2 teaspoons ground cumin

2 teaspoons ground coriander

½ teaspoon chilli powder

½ teaspoon turmeric

½–1 teaspoon salt, or to taste

You can buy ready-made samosas – fried cone-shaped pastries usually filled with vegetables – at every corner shop in India. But the homemade version is much nicer and can be made in a range of sizes, depending on whether you want to serve them as cocktail nibbles or as a starter or light lunch. Serve these savoury vegan versions with Green chutney (page 161).

सब्ज़ी समोसे

VEGETABLE SAMOSAS

To make the filling, cook the vegetables of your choice in a medium saucepan of boiling salted water over a medium heat until they are just tender. As a guide, cook the potato for 4 minutes; add the carrot, corn and sweet potato and cook for a further 2 minutes; then add the beans, peas and cauliflower and cook for a final 2 minutes. Drain.

Heat the oil in a large frying pan over a medium heat. Add the cumin, coriander, chilli powder, turmeric, salt and cooked vegetables; mix together well and cook for about 1 minute.

Remove from the heat and allow to cool.

Cut the sheets of pastry into ovals: make ovals 7.5 cm (3 in) in length for small samosas and 15 cm (6 in) in length for large samosas. Cut each oval in half across the width of the oval – you now have narrow hemispherical pastry shapes. Fold the corners on the straight side of each hemisphere inwards. Lightly moisten the edges of each hemisphere with water, then bring the two edges to meet, pinch them together and shape the pastry into a cone. Place a little of the filling in each cone, then fold over the top of the pastry to cover the filling and seal the samosa.

Heat the oil in a wok or deep-fryer to 180°C (350°F; see page 27). Fry a few samosas at a time until light brown and the pastry is cooked – about 5 minutes for small samosas and 7 minutes for large samosas. Drain on kitchen towels and serve hot.

NOTE: Most ready-made shortcrust pastry is made with oil; if butter is included in the ingredients, it will be clearly specified.

A really retro recipe, this dish is one of colonial India's favourite soups and it is still served in stuffy clubs and dingy hill station hotels. Full of lovely aromatic flavours, this British-influenced 'pepper water' is fabulously fragrant and will warm up the coldest evening. A true jewel in the Raj culinary crown!

PREPARATION TIME
30 minutes

COOKING TIME
80 minutes

SERVES
4

दाल और सब्ज़ी का मुलगुशोरबा
MULLIGATAWNY SOUP

In a large saucepan or stockpot, combine the onion, ginger and garlic pastes, lentils or peas, carrot or turnip, pumpkin, sweet potato, cinnamon, curry leaves and turmeric with 800 ml (27 fl oz) water. Bring to a boil over a medium heat, then lower the heat and simmer for 1 hour.

When the lentils are soft, stir in the coconut milk, tomato, cumin, coriander, fenugreek, and salt and pepper to taste, and cook for 15 minutes. Stir in the lime juice and cook for a further 5 minutes.

Serve hot, garnished with a little cooked rice if you have it available, fried onions and lemon or lime wedges.

1 small onion, sliced

1 teaspoon ginger paste (page 25)

1 teaspoon garlic paste (page 25)

100 g (3½ oz/⅓ cup) split red lentils (masoor dal) or yellow split peas

2 carrots or 1 turnip, peeled and diced

100 g (3½ oz/⅔ cup) pumpkin, peeled and diced

1 sweet potato, peeled and diced

2.5–5 cm (1–2 in) cinnamon stick

12 curry leaves

1 teaspoon turmeric

250 ml (8½ fl oz/1 cup) coconut milk

4 ripe tomatoes, chopped, or 400 g (14 oz) tin diced tomatoes, drained

2 teaspoons each cumin and coriander seeds, roasted and ground (page 18)

¼ teaspoon fenugreek seeds, roasted and ground (page 18)

salt and freshly ground black pepper to taste

2 tablespoons lime juice

cooked rice (optional) to garnish

fried onions (page 191) to garnish

lemon or lime wedges to garnish

PREPARATION TIME
15 minutes

COOKING TIME
40 minutes

SERVES
4

Soups were not traditionally served in India as a first course until the arrival of the British. However, soup-like drinks, both hot and cold, were sometimes served in tumblers throughout the meal. North Indian soups are sometimes called shorba, which can also be another name for a thick sauce or gravy. This shorba – a combination of sweet and hot spices, mushrooms and coconut – is a really nourishing soup. Serve it hot with fresh, crusty bread.

ढींगरी और नारयिल का शोरबा

MUSHROOM AND COCONUT SHORBA

30 g (1 oz) vegan butter
2 onions, sliced
360 g (12½ oz) button or cap mushrooms, cleaned and sliced
pinch of white pepper
½ teaspoon fennel seeds, ground
1 cm (½ in) cinnamon stick, ground
½ teaspoon cumin seeds, ground
2 green cardamom pods
½ teaspoon coriander seeds
250 ml (8½ fl oz/1 cup) coconut milk
1 teaspoon ginger paste (page 25)
125 ml (4 fl oz/½ cup) vegan thickened cream
4 makrut (kaffir lime) leaves
½–1 teaspoon salt, or to taste

Heat the butter in a large saucepan over a medium heat. Sauté the onion for about 7 minutes, or until translucent. Add the mushrooms, white pepper, fennel, cinnamon, cumin, cardamom pods, coriander and 125 ml (4 fl oz/½ cup) of the coconut milk. Cook for 10 minutes over a low heat. Remove from the heat and allow to cool a little.

Puree the mixture in a food processor or with a hand-held blender. Return the puree to the saucepan, and stir through the remaining coconut milk, the ginger paste, cream and makrut leaves. Cook over a medium heat for about 6 minutes, or until the soup is heated through. Add the salt and serve hot.

PREPARATION TIME
40 minutes

COOKING TIME
20 minutes

SERVES
4

---

150 g (5½ oz) vegan butter
2 tablespoons ginger paste (page 25)
6 ripe tomatoes, diced, or 600 g (1.5 x 400 g tins) tinned diced tomatoes, drained
2 tablespoons garlic paste (page 25)
4 large potatoes, peeled, boiled and roughly mashed
2 teaspoons chilli powder
½–1 teaspoon salt, or to taste
small handful coriander (cilantro) leaves, chopped, plus extra to serve
1 teaspoon garam masala (page 20)
8 small bread rolls, sliced in half crosswise
lemon wedges to serve

The Bollywood crowd queue up at Mumbai's specialist cafes and street carts for this favourite snack – a silky vegetable dip served with buttered toasted rolls. The Portuguese introduced yeast-type breads to western India in the sixteenth century. *Pao* refers to small loaves of bread, and *bhajee* is a selection of vegetables cooked on a hotplate with tomatoes and butter.

पाओ भाजी

PAO BHAJEE

Heat a heavy-based frying pan or a barbecue hotplate to a medium heat. Melt 75 g (2¾ oz) of the butter, then add the ginger paste and cook, stirring, for 5–10 seconds. Stir in the tomato and garlic paste and cook for about 8–10 minutes, or until the tomato has softened. Add the potato, chilli powder and salt and cook over a medium heat, stirring continuously, for about 10 minutes. Add the coriander and finally the garam masala and stir to mix through. Transfer the bhajee to a heatproof bowl.

Melt the remaining butter in the pan or on the hotplate. Add the bread rolls, cut side down, and cook over a medium heat for about 4–6 minutes, or until they are brown and have soaked up the melted butter.

Serve the bread rolls topped with the bhajee and extra chopped coriander, plus the lemon wedges on the side. Alternatively, serve the bhajee in a bowl with the rolls on a serving platter, for scooping up the vegetable dip.

Walk into a South Indian canteen or cafe during the early part of the day and you will be greeted by the sight of large hotplates with many variations of the uthappam being cooked to order. Uthappams – the word is derived from *appam*, which is a rice pancake – are South India's fantastic breakfast and brunch dish. Top these fermented rice and lentil pancakes with grated raw beetroot, or chopped spinach, tomatoes or mushrooms for an interesting alternative. Don't be put off by the time it takes to make the batter – once made, it can be left in the refrigerator for a week.

प्याज उत्तपम
ONION UTHAPPAMS

PREPARATION TIME
15 minutes (plus soaking and fermentation time)

COOKING TIME
30 minutes

SERVES
4

---

30 g (1 oz) vegan ghee or vegan butter, or 2 tablespoons vegetable or sunflower oil

Coconut chutney (page 158) to serve

BATTER

225 g (8 oz/1 cup) parboiled (converted) rice or other short-grain rice

75 g (2½ oz) basmati rice or other long-grain rice

150 g (5½ oz/⅔ cup) split white lentils (white urad dal)

½ teaspoon fenugreek seeds

1 red (Spanish) onion, chopped

2 green chillies, chopped

large handful coriander (cilantro) leaves, chopped

½–1 teaspoon salt, or to taste

To make the batter, rinse the parboiled and basmati rice and the lentils in cold water, then drain. Put in a large bowl with the fenugreek seeds and 2 litres (68 fl oz/8 cups) water, cover and soak overnight.

Drain the rice, lentils and fenugreek seeds, then process in a food processor to form a smooth batter that has the consistency of a thick soup. Pour into a clean large bowl, cover and keep in a warm place for 8–12 hours to allow the batter to ferment. When it is ready, it will have little bubbles on the surface and a slightly sour smell.

Add the onion, chilli, coriander and salt to the batter and mix thoroughly.

Heat a heavy-based non-stick frying pan over a medium heat for about 2 minutes. Pour a small ladleful of batter into the pan and swirl it around to cover the base of the pan and form a thin pancake. Cook for about 4 minutes, or until bubbles appear on the surface. Add a little ghee, butter or oil around the edges of the pancake, then turn and cook the other side for a further 3 minutes, until golden brown and crunchy on the outside. Remove from the pan and serve with the coconut chutney.

PREPARATION TIME
30 minutes

COOKING TIME
30 minutes

SERVES
4 (makes 8–10)

---

75 g (2¾ oz) finely shredded white or red cabbage

1 tablespoon finely chopped onion

2 tablespoons finely chopped coriander (cilantro) leaves

1 teaspoon finely chopped green chilli

½ teaspoon turmeric

110 g (4 oz/1 cup) besan (chickpea flour)

½–1 teaspoon salt, or to taste

vegetable or sunflower oil for deep-frying

Coconut chutney (page 158) to serve

A very popular snack in Mumbai and its surrounding regions, bondas are round fritters made with besan (chickpea flour) and potatoes. Sold from street carts or udipi cafes (vegetarian working-mens' canteens known for great-value, basic food), bondas are easily made at home. This version is not so well known but is delicious with the added crunch of cabbage.

पत्तागोभी बोडा

CABBAGE BONDAS

Mix together the cabbage, onion, coriander, chilli, turmeric, besan and salt in a large bowl. Add 60 ml (2 fl oz/¼ cup) water, 1 tablespoon at a time, and stir to combine until the mixture holds together firmly. (The amount of water required will depend on the type of besan you use, as some besans retain more liquid than others.) With wet hands, shape the mixture into flattened patties, about 1 cm (½ in) thick and 3 cm (1¼ in) in diameter.

Heat the oil in a wok or deep-fryer to 180°C (350°F; see page 27). Deep-fry the patties, a few at a time, for about 4 minutes, or until crisp and golden brown. Drain on kitchen towels and serve with the coconut chutney.

NOTE: The mixture can be stored in the refrigerator for up to 12 hours. During this time, water will seep out of the salted cabbage and make the mixture runny, so you may find that you do not need to add extra water before forming the mixture into patties.

There is a huge repertoire of Indian kabab recipes, but this unique, melt-in-the-mouth North Indian version, made from drained plain vegan yoghurt, is outstanding. Yoghurt is a very popular ingredient throughout India and can take a starring role, as this recipe demonstrates. Serve the patties with a green salad and Tomato chutney (page 166). They are also good as a starter or as part of an Indian banquet.

दही के कबाब

DAHI KE KABABS

PREPARATION TIME
15 minutes (plus draining time)

COOKING TIME
10 minutes

SERVES
3–4 (makes 6–8)
Serves 3–4 / Makes 6–8

1 kg (2 lb 3 oz/4 cups) vegan plain yoghurt

1 teaspoon finely chopped green chilli

1 tablespoon finely chopped coriander (cilantro) leaves

55 g (2 oz/½ cup) besan (chickpea flour)

½–1 teaspoon salt, or to taste

60 ml (2 fl oz/¼ cup) vegetable or sunflower oil

Put the yoghurt in the middle of a clean square of muslin (cheesecloth) resting in a bowl or container. Bring the corners in to meet at the centre and tie in a knot. Hang the bundle containing the yoghurt from a hook, put a container underneath to catch the draining fluid, and leave to drain for 6–8 hours. In warmer weather, hang the bundle in the refrigerator.

Tip the drained yoghurt into a large bowl. Add the chilli, coriander, besan and salt, and mix well. With wet hands, shape the mixture into small patties about 2.5 cm (1 in) in diameter. (You should make 6–8 patties from this amount of mixture.)

Heat the oil in a heavy-based frying pan over a medium heat. Cook the patties, a few at a time, for about 2 minutes on each side, or until golden brown and crusty on the outside. Drain on kitchen towels and serve hot.

PREPARATION TIME
15 minutes

COOKING TIME
25 minutes

SERVES
4 (makes 12)

---

3 potatoes, skins left on

6 banana chillies

½ teaspoon chilli powder

½ teaspoon ground amchur

½–1 teaspoon salt, or to taste

vegetable or sunflower oil for deep-frying

BATTER

110 g (4 oz/1 cup) besan (chickpea flour)

½ teaspoon turmeric

½ teaspoon chilli powder

1 teaspoon ajwain seeds

½–1 teaspoon salt, or to taste

Today, India produces almost every variety of chilli available, but chillies were in fact only introduced there in the sixteenth century. Chilli is mainly used to impart that addictive hot sensation to food, but some recipes have evolved with chilli as the star ingredient. This recipe is one of them, and despite the fact that you are biting into a chilli, these pakoras are not very hot because banana chillies are mild and the seeds are removed. Serve with Green chutney (page 161) as a snack or as an accompaniment to Vegetable khichadi (page 104).

मर्चि और आलू के पकौड़े

BANANA CHILLI AND POTATO PAKORAS

Cook the potatoes in a covered saucepan of boiling salted water over a medium heat for about 15 minutes, or until cooked through. Drain well, then leave until cool enough to handle. Peel and roughly mash. (You should have the equivalent of about 230 g (8 oz/1 cup) of mashed potato.)

While the potato is cooling, carefully cut the banana chillies in half lengthwise and remove the seeds.

Mix together the potato, chilli powder, amchur and salt in a medium bowl. Stuff each chilli half with this mixture.

To make the batter, mix the besan, turmeric, chilli powder, ajwain seeds and salt in a medium bowl. Add about 375 ml (12½ fl oz/ 1½ cups) water gradually, until the batter has the correct consistency – it should coat the back of the spoon and gently drip down. (The amount of water required to achieve this consistency will depend on the type of besan you use, as some besans retain more liquid than others.)

Heat the oil in a wok or deep-fryer to 180°C (350°F; see page 27). Carefully dip the stuffed chillies in the batter, then deep-fry them for about 5 minutes or until golden brown and crisp. Drain on kitchen towels and serve immediately.

PREPARATION TIME
15 minutes

COOKING TIME
20 minutes

SERVES
4

- 8 large Swiss brown mushrooms or other flat/field mushrooms, cleaned and stalks removed
- 1 tablespoon crushed black peppercorns
- 2 tablespoons sesame oil
- 30 g (1 oz) vegan ghee or 2 tablespoons vegetable or sunflower oil
- ¼ red (Spanish) onion, finely chopped
- ½ teaspoon fresh ginger, finely crushed
- 150 g (5½ oz/1 cup) fresh or frozen peas
- ½ teaspoon turmeric
- 2 tablespoons chopped coriander (cilantro) leaves
- 1 teaspoon finely chopped green chilli
- ¼ teaspoon chilli powder
- ½–1 teaspoon salt, or to taste
- 4 tablespoons fresh breadcrumbs
- lemon wedges to serve

Breakfast in India is never boring! This stuffed mushroom and green pea dish is fresh and filling. It can also be served on a bed of Crispy straw potatoes (page 127), a slice of toasted sourdough or Turkish flatbread dribbled with good-quality olive oil, or with Pooris (page 132) for a proper Indian breakfast.

ढींगरी भरवां, मटर और डबल रोटी चूर

GRILLED SWISS BROWN MUSHROOMS WITH SPICED BREADCRUMBS AND GREEN PEAS

Preheat the grill (broiler) to a medium heat or preheat the oven to 200°C (390°F).

Put the mushrooms, pepper and sesame oil in a large bowl and stir carefully to coat well. Set aside for 5 minutes.

Grill the mushrooms for 6 minutes, or roast them in the oven for 7–8 minutes.

Heat the ghee or oil in a large frying pan over a medium heat. Add the onion and sauté till light brown. Stir in the ginger, then the peas, turmeric, coriander, green chilli, chilli powder, salt and breadcrumbs. Cook for a further 5 minutes. Fill each mushroom with some of this mixture and serve with lemon wedges.

These crispy, breadcrumb-coated, soft, beetrooty patties have the crunch of peanuts and the firm, sweet bite of sultanas. They are a must at a Bengali wedding. Imagine the wedding guests at long tables, eating off banana leaves, the waiters bearing baskets of freshly cooked beetroot (beet 'chops'). A chef once shared his secret ingredient for this dish with me: he used beer instead of milk for the coating! Serve as a cocktail snack or as part of an Indian meal.

चुकंदर चॉप

BEETROOT AND VEGETABLE 'CHOPS'

PREPARATION TIME
40 minutes

COOKING TIME
15 minutes

SERVES
4 (makes 8–10)

- 1 small beetroot (beet), peeled and quartered
- 1 potato, peeled and quartered
- 2 carrots, peeled and thickly sliced
- 60 g (2 oz) shelled fresh or frozen peas
- 2 tablespoons unsalted raw peanuts
- 2 tablespoons sultanas (golden raisins)
- 1 green chilli, chopped
- 1 tablespoon garam masala (page 20)
- ½–1 teaspoon salt, or to taste
- 150 g (5½ oz/1 cup) plain (all-purpose) flour, divided
- 125 ml (4 fl oz/½ cup) vegan milk or beer
- 75 g (2¾ oz) panko breadcrumbs
- vegetable or sunflower oil for deep-frying

Put the beetroot in a small saucepan of boiling salted water and cook over a medium heat for 20 minutes, or until cooked through. Drain well, then roughly mash. Meanwhile, put the potato and carrot in a medium saucepan of boiling salted water and cook over a medium heat for 8 minutes. Add the peas, bring back to a boil and cook for 2 minutes. Drain well, then roughly mash.

Put the mashed beetroot, potato, carrot and peas in a large bowl. Stir in the peanuts, sultanas, chilli, garam masala and salt and mix thoroughly. With your hands, shape the mixture into egg-shaped patties. (You should make 8–10 patties with this amount of mixture.)

Put 75g (2 ¾ oz/½ cup) of the flour into a bowl and gradually add enough water to make a thick batter. Lightly beat the batter with the milk or beer in a shallow bowl.

Put the remaining 75g (2 ¾ oz/½ cup) of flour on a large plate and the breadcrumbs on a separate large plate.

Roll each patty in the flour to lightly coat, then dip the patty in the batter mixture to cover completely. Allow any excess to drip off before rolling the patty in the breadcrumbs, pressing down firmly to make sure it is well coated. Repeated with remaining patties.

Heat the oil in a wok or deep-fryer to 180°C (350°F; see page 27). Deep-fry a few of the patties at a time for about 4 minutes, or until golden brown. Repeat with the remaining patties. Drain on kitchen towels and serve hot.

Upma, meaning salt and flour, is a recipe that originates from the south of India. This is a great dish for breakfast, brunch or a light lunch. The semolina resembles a flaky, light polenta dish with the added flavour of spices, and is delicious teamed with Sambar dal (page 100) and Coconut chutney (page 158).

PREPARATION TIME
15 minutes

COOKING TIME
10 minutes

SERVES
4

उपमा
UPMA

Heat the ghee or oil in a large frying pan over a medium heat. Stir in the mustard seeds, split white lentils and yellow split peas, asafoetida and curry leaves, and cook until the mustard seeds start to crackle. Immediately add the onion, ginger and chilli and sauté for about 5 minutes, stirring occasionally.

Add the turmeric and semolina and stir continuously, until the semolina is well coated with the mixture. Add 250 ml (8½ fl oz/1 cup) water and the salt and cook, stirring vigorously, for 5 minutes, or until the semolina is cooked and has absorbed all the water. Stir the lemon juice and coriander through the semolina mixture and serve hot.

30 g (1 oz) vegan ghee or 2 tablespoons vegetable or sunflower oil

1 teaspoon black mustard seeds

1 teaspoon split white lentils (white urad dal)

½ teaspoon yellow split peas

1 teaspoon asafoetida

1 tablespoon curry leaves

1 tablespoon chopped onion

1 teaspoon finely chopped fresh ginger

1 teaspoon finely chopped green chilli

½ teaspoon turmeric

125 g (4½ oz/1 cup) semolina

½–1 teaspoon salt, or to taste

1 tablespoon lemon juice

1 tablespoon finely chopped coriander (cilantro) leaves

PREPARATION TIME
15 minutes (plus soaking time)

COOKING TIME
15 minutes

SERVES
4 (makes 8)

- 115 g (4 oz) split red lentils (masoor dal), rinsed and drained
- 1 tablespoon finely chopped onion
- 1 teaspoon finely chopped green chilli
- ½ teaspoon red chilli powder
- 1 tablespoon finely chopped fresh ginger
- 1 tablespoon black pepper, crushed
- ½ teaspoon asafoetida
- 1½ teaspoons salt, or to taste
- vegetable or sunflower oil for deep-frying
- lime wedges to serve

Wadas are fried lentil or vegetable dumplings. They originate from western and southern India and are usually served as a snack or cocktail nibble. These wadas go well with Coconut chutney (page 158) or can become a light lunch or brunch with the addition of Sambar dal (page 100).

मसूर दाल वड़ा

MASOOR DAL WADAS

Put the lentils in a medium-sized bowl, cover with water and soak for 2 hours. Drain, then transfer to a food processor and crush coarsely.

Transfer the lentil mixture to a clean bowl and add the onion, green chilli and chilli powder, and mix well. With wet hands, shape the mixture into eight small, flat patties, about 2.5–3.5 cm (1–1½ in) in diameter.

Heat the oil in a wok or deep-fryer to a medium heat of 180°C (350°F; see page 27). Deep-fry the patties in two batches for about 5 minutes, or until crisp and cooked. Drain on kitchen towels and serve hot with a squeeze of fresh lime.

PREPARATION TIME
7 minutes

COOKING TIME
20 minutes

SERVES
4 (makes 16)

---

2 large onions, sliced

55 g (2 oz/½ cup) besan (chickpea flour)

pinch of chilli powder

pinch of turmeric

2 teaspoons white vinegar

½–1 teaspoon salt, or to taste

vegetable or sunflower oil for deep-frying

In Gujarat, pakoras, or vegetable fritters, are known as *bhajees* or *bhajias*. They are quick to cook and fun to eat as a starter or a cocktail bite. Serve these with Tamarind and ginger chutney (page 160) or Lime juice chutney (page 168).

प्याज भाजी

ONION BHAJEES

Mix together the onion, besan, chilli powder, turmeric, vinegar and salt in a large bowl.

Add 60–125 ml (2–4 fl oz/¼–½ cup) water to the mixture gradually, 1 tablespoon at a time, and mix until the besan coats the onion. There should be just enough besan mixture to hold the onion slices together. (The amount of water required to achieve this consistency will depend on the type of besan you use, as some besans retain more liquid than others. Do not add too much water as the bhajees will disintegrate when fried.)

Heat the oil in a wok or deep-fryer to 180°C (350°; see page 27). Deep-fry a few bhajees at a time for about 6–8 minutes, or until crisp and golden brown. Repeat with the remaining bhajees. Drain on kitchen towels and serve hot.

Vegetable biryani सब्जी बिरियानी	64
Green bean thoran हरी बीन थोरन	67
Corn takatak मकई टकाटक	68
Kum kum tamatar कुम कुम टमाटर	70
Pumpkin with panch phoron कुमरो पंचफोरन	73
Mixed vegetable navratan curry नवरतन कारी	74
Sweet potato and turnip bhurta शकरकंद और शलजम का भरता	75
Vegetable medley with panch phoron पंच फोरोनर चरचारी	76
Vegetable chakka सब्ज़ी चक्का	77
Spinach with tofu पालक टोफू	79
Green peas with ginger and lemon हरी मटर अदरक और नींबू के साथ	81
Smoky eggplant bhurta ढुंगरी बैंगन भरता	82
Tomatoes filled with mushrooms and figs ढींगरी और अंजीर से भरे टमाटर	83
Okra do pyaz भिंडी दो प्याज़	86
Karahi-style baby spinach and mushrooms करहै पालकौर ढींगरी	88
Spicy pumpkin हलवाई का कद्दू	90
Jackfruit kohlapuri कटहल कोहलापुरी	91
Vegetable moilee सब्ज़ी की मोली	92
Cauliflower masala फूलगोभी मसाला	93
Baked mustard broccoli सरसो ब्रोकोली	94

India is home to the world's largest vegetarian population, with 60–70 per cent consuming an entirely meat-free diet. As a result, wonderful vegan and vegetarian dishes, ranging from the simplest to the most elaborate, appear in the homes of both the rich and the poor, and in restaurants throughout the nation. Just one or two spices are needed to enhance the distinctive flavour of individual vegetables, whether it be the humble potato, a sweet pumpkin (winter squash) or the more exotic okra.

Traditionally, vegetables and pulses are eaten together with other dishes as part of a shared meal. Rice dishes such as Vegetable biryani (page 64) and Mushroom and chickpea pulao (page 121) often feature alongside wet and drier vegetable curries and dals, as well as simple side dishes, such as Green bean thoran (page 67) or Pumpkin with panch phoron (page 73).

Nuts play an important part in vegetable recipes. Used whole, crushed coarsely, powdered or in milk, cream and paste, cashews, walnuts, pine nuts, almonds and pistachios can add a delicious flavour and creaminess. They are also good thickening agents and provide a gluten-free substitute for many flours.

The dishes in this chapter can be eaten either as standalone meals with rice or bread, or as part of a larger feast. Try pairing them with other recipes in this book and see which flavours you like best. There are no rules!

VEGETABLE DISHES

PREPARATION TIME
25 minutes

COOKING TIME
30 minutes

SERVES
4

- 60 g (2 oz) vegan ghee or 60 ml (2 fl oz/¼ cup) vegetable or sunflower oil
- 2 green chillies
- 1 teaspoon whole mace
- 5 cloves
- 5 green cardamom pods
- 1 teaspoon black cumin seeds
- 1 small onion, sliced
- 225 g (8 oz) basmati rice or other long-grain rice, washed and drained
- 150 g (5½ oz/1 cup) diced mixed seasonal vegetables, choosing 4–6 of the following:
  - ½ small eggplant (aubergine)
  - 2 Swiss brown or field mushrooms, cleaned
  - 2 cauliflower florets
  - 1 carrot, peeled
  - 40 g (1½ oz/¼ cup) frozen peas
  - 6 green beans, trimmed
  - 1 large potato, peeled
  - 1 tomato
- 60 g (2 oz/¼ cup) vegan plain yoghurt
- 1 tablespoon chopped coriander (cilantro) leaves
- 1 tablespoon chopped mint leaves
- ½–1 teaspoon salt, or to taste
- 1 tablespoon saffron infusion (page 21)
- unsalted roasted cashew nuts to garnish
- sultanas (golden raisins) to garnish

With its origins in Persia (present-day Iran), biryani is essentially a special rice dish flavoured with saffron and spices. Eleventh-century Mughals loved their rice pilafs, and these evolved into the more elaborate biryani with the addition of spices and distinctive regional ingredients. Vegetable versions are popular in India and may be served on their own, with nothing more than Boondi raita (page 151) or Dahi chutney (page 158).

सब्ज़ी बरियानी

VEGETABLE BIRYANI

Heat the ghee or oil in a large heavy-based saucepan over a medium heat. Stir in the chillies, mace, cloves, cardamom pods and black cumin seeds and cook for 5 seconds. Immediately add the onion and sauté, stirring occasionally, for about 5 minutes, or until golden brown.

Add the rice and stir until each grain is coated with the mixture. Add the diced mixed seasonal vegetables and the yoghurt, coriander and mint, and stir to mix through.

Stir in 625 ml (21 fl oz/2½ cups) boiling water plus the salt, then cover and cook over a high heat until it comes to a boil. Reduce the heat to low and simmer gently for about 20 minutes, or until the rice is almost cooked.

Carefully pour the saffron infusion in one place on top of the almost-cooked rice but do not stir. Cover and continue cooking for a further 15 minutes, or until all the liquid is absorbed and the vegetables are tender.

If you wish, gently stir the biryani just before serving – this is done to produce the trademark yellow and white grains of a biryani, but you must do it very carefully to avoid breaking up the rice grains. Garnish with the cashew nuts and sultanas, and serve.

PREPARATION TIME
10 minutes

COOKING TIME
15 minutes

SERVES
4

1½ tablespoons vegetable or sunflower oil

1 whole dried red chilli

¼ teaspoon fenugreek seeds

½ teaspoon black mustard seeds

6 curry leaves

1 teaspoon ginger paste (page 25)

350 g (12½ oz) green beans, trimmed and diced

½–1 teaspoon salt, or to taste

25 g (1 oz) shredded (grated dried) coconut or 40 g (1½ oz) freshly grated coconut

---

In the temples of South India, the cooks have created a style of cooking that pays attention to the physical and spiritual wellbeing of the individual. The food is used as a sacrifice to the gods and is also distributed to pilgrims, temple devotees and the poor. This dish is one of these recipes. In this version, the taste of coconut, curry leaves and spices adds another dimension to the sweetness of green beans.

हरी बीन थोरन
GREEN BEAN THORAN

Heat the oil in a large wok or frying pan over a medium heat. Stir in the chilli, fenugreek seeds, black mustard seeds and curry leaves and cook until the mustard seeds start to crackle. Immediately add the ginger paste and beans and sauté, stirring, for about 1 minute. Stir in the salt, then reduce the heat to low, cover and cook for about 15 minutes, stirring occasionally, until the beans are tender but not overcooked.

Stir in the coconut and cook for a further 2 minutes, then serve.

NOTE: This dish can also be served as a warm salad, accompanied by steamed basmati rice or other long-grain rice, Pooris (page 132) or Parathas (page 134).

Making a takatak involves cooking at high temperatures on a hotplate or barbecue plate, and breaking up the ingredients with a metal spatula, the sound of which – 'takatak'– gives its name to the dish. This method of cooking originated in north-west India and is also well known in Pakistan, where many different vegetables are used. Serve this corn and tomato dish with fresh Indian bread.

PREPARATION TIME
15 minutes

COOKING TIME
20 minutes

SERVES
4

मकई टकाटक

CORN TAKATAK

15 g (½ oz) vegan ghee, or 2 teaspoons vegetable or sunflower oil and 10 g (¼ oz) vegan butter
pinch of ajwain seeds
1 tablespoon chopped onion
1 teaspoon chopped fresh ginger
250 g (9 oz/1 cup) tomato puree (pureed tomatoes) or 3 tomatoes, skin and seeds removed, pureed (see Notes)
1 tablespoon tomato paste (concentrated puree)
1 teaspoon ground coriander
1 teaspoon dried fenugreek leaves
½ teaspoon chilli powder
½ –1 teaspoon salt, or to taste
200 g (7 oz/1 cup) corn kernels cut from the cob
2 tablespoons chopped coriander (cilantro) leaves

Heat the ghee or oil and butter in a large heavy-based frying pan or on a barbecue hotplate over a high heat. Add the ajwain seeds, then immediately add the onion and sauté, stirring frequently, for about 2 minutes, or until light brown. Stir in the ginger and sauté for 1 minute.

Add the tomato puree, tomato paste, ground coriander, fenugreek leaves, chilli powder and salt and cook for about 1 minute, stirring continuously.

Stir in the corn, reduce the heat to low and simmer for about 5 minutes, until tender. Scatter over the chopped coriander and serve hot.

NOTES: If you are using whole tomatoes to make the tomato puree, score a cross in the base of each tomato. Put in a heatproof bowl and cover with boiling water. Leave for 30 seconds, then transfer to cold water. When cool enough to handle, peel the skin away, starting from the cross. Cut the tomato in half crosswise, scoop out the seeds with a teaspoon and discard. Process the tomato flesh in a food processor to form a puree.

This recipe uses the *bhuna* technique (see page 191).

An innovative and delicious recipe for special occasions, kum kum tamatar is a unique dish, that uses the *bhuna* technique (see page 191). Serve it with Naan (page 128) or Pooris (page 132), or as part of an Indian feast.

PREPARATION TIME
15 minutes

COOKING TIME
45 minutes

SERVES
4

कुम कुम टमाटर
KUM KUM TAMATAR

1 eggplant (aubergine)

4 large or 8 medium vine-ripened or ripe tomatoes

1 tablespoon mustard oil

1 tablespoon finely chopped onion

1 teaspoon ginger paste (page 25)

1 teaspoon garlic paste (page 25)

1 tablespoon finely chopped green chilli

1 tablespoon finely chopped coriander (cilantro) leaves

½ teaspoon turmeric

½–1 teaspoon salt, or to taste

1 tablespoon saffron infusion (page 21)

1 teaspoon kewra essence (see Note)

coriander (cilantro) leaves to garnish

ROGINI SAUCE

60 g (2 oz) vegan ghee or 60 ml (2 fl oz/¼ cup) vegetable or sunflower oil

½ teaspoon ginger paste (page 25)

½ teaspoon garlic paste (page 25)

1 teaspoon ground coriander

½ teaspoon turmeric

½ teaspoon chilli powder

40 g (1½ oz/¼ cup) raw cashew nuts

1 onion, sliced

190 ml (6½ fl oz/¾ cup) vegan thickened cream

2 tablespoons tomato paste (concentrated puree)

To make the rogini sauce, heat the ghee or oil in a large frying pan over a medium heat. Sauté the ginger and garlic pastes for about 30 seconds. Add the remaining sauce ingredients with 250 ml (8½ fl oz/1 cup) water. Stir and heat through, reduce the heat to low and simmer gently for 20 minutes. Remove from the heat, allow to cool, then puree in a food processor.

Meanwhile, cook the eggplant in a heavy-based frying pan or chargrill pan over a medium heat, or under the grill (broiler), for about 20 minutes, or until soft and the skin is charred (turn the eggplant only once or twice during cooking). Remove from the pan and leave until cool. Cut in half (discarding the skin), scoop out the flesh, chop roughly and set aside.

Cut the tops off the tomatoes and discard. Scoop out the pulp, reserving this and the hollowed-out tomato shells separately.

Heat the mustard oil in a separate frying pan over a medium heat. Sauté the onion, stirring occasionally, for about 3 minutes, or until golden brown. Add the ginger and garlic pastes and cook, stirring, for 1 minute. Add the chilli, chopped coriander, turmeric, reserved eggplant and tomato pulp and salt. Mix, then cover and cook for 5 minutes. Remove from the heat.

Using a spoon, fill the hollowed-out tomatoes with the tomato and eggplant mixture, pressing it in firmly.

Return the pureed rogini sauce to the frying pan and heat through over a low heat. Stir through the saffron infusion, kewra essence and salt.

Carefully put the stuffed tomatoes in the sauce and simmer gently over a low heat for about 20 minutes, until they are soft. Garnish with coriander leaves and serve hot.

NOTE: Kewra essence (available in Indian grocery stores) is extracted from the keora flower and is used to flavour rich Mughal curries and rice dishes. It is concentrated and should be used sparingly.

PREPARATION TIME
15 minutes

COOKING TIME
30 minutes

SERVES
4

1 tablespoon mustard oil
1 dried whole red chilli
1 teaspoon panch phoron (page 21)
500 g (1 lb 2 oz) pumpkin (winter squash), such as butternut, Japanese or kent, peeled and diced
½ teaspoon sugar (optional)
½–1 teaspoon salt, or to taste

Bengal is the only region in India where food is traditionally served in a succession of courses. First, vegetables are served with steamed rice, followed by dal and curries. This dish of pumpkin with panch phoron is a typical Bengali recipe – a simply cooked vegetable with the five spices found in panch phoron highlighting the vegetable's natural flavours. Serve with other curries and steamed rice.

कुमरो पंचफोरन

PUMPKIN WITH PANCH PHORON

Heat the mustard oil in a small wok or frying pan over a medium heat. Stir in the chilli and panch phoron and cook until the panch phoron starts to crackle.

Immediately stir in the pumpkin, sugar, if using, and salt. Add 125 ml (4 fl oz/½ cup) water, then reduce the heat to low, cover and cook, stirring occasionally, for about 30 minutes, or until the pumpkin is soft. Serve hot.

This dish takes its name from the nine famous wise men of Akbar's Mughal court in fourteenth-century Agra. *Navratan* literally means 'nine gems', and many dishes, which usually comprised nine ingredients, were named after these nine wise courtiers. This recipe is an easy, everyday vegetable curry with great flavours and textures, using both root and green vegetables. Serve it as a vegan main course or as part of an Indian meal with Pulao rice (page 120) or fresh Chapattis (page 131), Pooris (page 132) or Parathas (page 134).

नवरतन कारी

MIXED VEGETABLE NAVRATAN CURRY

PREPARATION TIME
20 minutes

COOKING TIME
40 minutes

SERVES
4

- 1 tablespoon ground cumin
- 1 tablespoon ground coriander
- 1 teaspoon turmeric
- 1 teaspoon chilli powder
- 2 tablespoons vegetable or sunflower oil
- 1 small potato, peeled and diced
- ½ small sweet potato, peeled and diced
- 1 small carrot, peeled and diced
- 1 small turnip, peeled and diced
- 150 g (5½ oz) pumpkin (winter squash), peeled and diced
- 2 cauliflower florets, each cut lengthwise into 8 pieces
- 100 g (3½ oz) shredded cabbage
- 6 green beans, trimmed and diced
- 40 g (1½ oz/¼ cup) shelled fresh or frozen peas
- 125 g (4½ oz/½ cup) tomato paste (concentrated puree)
- ½–1 teaspoon salt, or to taste
- coriander (cilantro) leaves to garnish

Mix the ground cumin and coriander, turmeric and chilli powder together with 60 ml (2 fl oz/¼ cup) water in a small bowl to make a paste.

Heat the oil in a large saucepan over a medium heat. Stir in the spice paste and cook for 5–10 seconds.

Add the potato, sweet potato, carrot and turnip with 375 ml (12½ fl oz/1½ cups) water and stir to mix through. Cover and cook over a medium heat for 25 minutes, or until the vegetables are three-quarters cooked.

Add the pumpkin, cauliflower, cabbage, beans, peas and tomato paste and stir to mix through. Reduce the heat to low, cover and cook for a further 15 minutes. Add salt to taste just before serving.

Garnish with the coriander leaves and serve hot.

NOTE: The total amount of vegetables used in this recipe should come to about 300 g (10½ oz/2 cups), once you've done all the peeling, dicing and shredding.

PREPARATION TIME
30 minutes

COOKING TIME
40 minutes

SERVES
4

---

2 large sweet potatoes, peeled and cut into 3 cm (1¼ in) pieces

2 turnips, peeled and cut into 3 cm (1¼ in) pieces

1 teaspoon vegetable or sunflower oil (optional)

15 g (½ oz) vegan ghee or 1 tablespoon vegetable or sunflower oil

1 dried whole red chilli

½ teaspoon fenugreek seeds

1 small onion, chopped

2 green chillies, seeds removed to reduce heat if desired, chopped

2 tomatoes, chopped

2 tablespoons chopped coriander (cilantro) leaves

1 teaspoon turmeric

½ –1 teaspoon salt, or to taste

Vegetable recipes in India are never boring. There are endless combinations of spices and cooking techniques, which vary from region to region. Even the meat eaters must have two or three vegetable dishes as part of their meal. This recipe is a very satisfying comfort food that can be eaten with anything. A *bhurta* is a rough mash, found in the north and east of India. It describes a special home-style method of cooking vegetables such as potatoes, eggplants (aubergines) and turnips. Serve this dish as part of a vegan meal.

शकरकंद और शलजम का भरता

SWEET POTATO AND TURNIP BHURTA

Place the sweet potato and turnip in a saucepan of boiling salted water and cook for 10 minutes, or until tender. Alternatively, put in a roasting tin, toss with the 1 teaspoon vegetable or sunflower oil and roast in an oven preheated to 180°C (350°F) for 20 minutes, or until tender. Roughly mash the sweet potato and turnip and set aside.

Heat the ghee or oil in a large frying pan over a medium heat. Stir in the dried red chilli and fenugreek seeds and cook for 5 seconds. Immediately add the onion and sauté, stirring occasionally, for about 5 minutes, or until golden brown.

Add the sweet potato and turnip mash, green chilli, tomato, coriander, turmeric and salt. Stir well to combine, then reduce the heat to low and cook gently, stirring frequently, for 5 minutes. Serve hot.

PREPARATION TIME
20 minutes

COOKING TIME
30 minutes

SERVES
4

---

1 tablespoon mustard or other vegetable oil

2 green chillies, slit to just below the stalk area, top and seeds left intact

1 teaspoon panch phoron (page 21)

1 large onion, sliced

1 tablespoon ginger paste (page 25)

1 tablespoon garlic paste (page 25)

1 teaspoon turmeric

½–1 teaspoon salt, or to taste

2 cauliflower florets, thinly sliced

100 g (3½ oz) pumpkin (winter squash), such as butternut, Japanese or kent, peeled and diced

1 zucchini (courgette), diced

65 g (2¼ oz) frozen peas

50 g (1¾ oz) baby spinach leaves

6 green beans, trimmed

¼ red, green or yellow capsicum (pepper), thinly sliced lengthwise

100 g (3½ oz) finely shredded white cabbage

lime wedges to serve

Some of the best recipes are never prepared in restaurants. This quick, healthy, easy and colourful dish from Bengal is a delicious example. The Indian five-spice mix panch phoron lifts this beautiful medley of seasonal vegetables into the realm of something special. Serve with steamed basmati or other long-grain rice and a lentil dish.

पंच फोरोनर चरचारी

VEGETABLE MEDLEY WITH PANCH PHORON

Heat the oil in a wok or large frying pan over a medium heat. If you are using mustard oil, wait until it is smoking (this gets rid of the pungent mustard flavour and releases a sweeter taste). Stir in the green chilli and panch phoron and cook until the mixture crackles. Immediately add the onion, ginger and garlic pastes, turmeric and salt, increase the heat to high and stir-fry for 2 minutes.

Add the cauliflower, pumpkin, zucchini, peas, spinach, beans, capsicum and cabbage and stir to mix through (see Note). Reduce the heat to low, cover and cook until the vegetables are tender. Serve hot, with lime wedges on the side for squeezing over.

NOTE: For a more colourful look, add the peas and spinach towards the end of cooking, rather than with the rest of the vegetables.

PREPARATION TIME
20 minutes

COOKING TIME
30 minutes

SERVES
4

1½ tablespoons mustard oil
1 teaspoon panch phoron (page 21)
2 dried whole red chillies
2 bay leaves
2.5 cm (1 in) cinnamon stick
2 cloves
1 teaspoon ginger paste (page 25)
1 small eggplant (aubergine), cut into 2.5 cm (1 in) pieces
200 g (7 oz) pumpkin (winter squash), peeled and cut into 2.5 cm (1 in) pieces
1 sweet potato, peeled and cut into 2.5 cm (1 in) pieces
1 zucchini (courgette), thickly sliced
4 cauliflower florets, each cut lengthwise into 4 pieces
12 green beans, trimmed and sliced into 2.5 cm (1 in) lengths
1 teaspoon sugar
1 teaspoon turmeric
½–1 teaspoon salt, or to taste

Chakka means six ingredients tossed together quickly. A Bengali favourite with slightly sweet overtones, this simple dish uses six different vegetables that complement each other in taste and texture. Make sure the vegetables are in their prime, preferably organic and in season, as in this recipe there is nowhere for them to hide. The whole spices accentuate the pure fresh flavours of the vegetables. Serve with steamed rice.

सब्जी चक्का

VEGETABLE CHAKKA

Heat the mustard oil in a wok or large frying pan over a medium heat. Stir in the panch phoron and chillies and cook until the mixture crackles. Immediately add the bay leaves, cinnamon, cloves and ginger paste and cook, stirring continuously, for 1 minute.

Add the eggplant, pumpkin, sweet potato, zucchini, cauliflower, beans, sugar, turmeric and salt. Stir to mix well, then cover with a tight-fitting lid and cook over the lowest heat possible for about 30 minutes or until the vegetables are tender. Only take the lid off to check and stir once during the cooking time. (This dish obtains the best taste when the vegetables cook in their own steam, without the addition of water. This can only be achieved when the lowest possible heat is used and when the lid is not opened more than once during cooking.) Serve hot.

NOTE: All the vegetables should be cut to the same size as much as possible. The prepared vegetables should come to about 600 g (1 lb 5 oz) in total before cooking.

PREPARATION TIME
15 minutes

COOKING TIME
20 minutes

SERVES
4

---

1 teaspoon vegetable or sunflower oil
1 small onion, chopped
1 teaspoon chopped fresh ginger
1 teaspoon chopped garlic
1 green chilli, chopped
1 teaspoon ground coriander
½ teaspoon turmeric
240 g (8½ oz) English spinach, washed, drained and chopped
1 teaspoon dried fenugreek leaves
250 g (9 oz) firm silken tofu, diced (see page 192)

This lovely green and fresh dish can be eaten on its own or teamed with a chickpea curry and a crunchy salad. English spinach will give the best flavour and texture here, but you can also use silverbeet (Swiss chard), kale or the Italian cavolo nero. Serve hot with Naan (page 128), Chapattis (page 131) or Parathas (page 134).

पालक टोफू

SPINACH WITH TOFU

Heat the oil in a large saucepan over a medium heat. Sauté the onion, stirring occasionally, for about 5–7 minutes, or until light brown.

Stir in the ginger, garlic and chilli and cook for 1 minute. Add the coriander, turmeric, spinach and fenugreek leaves and cook, stirring occasionally, for about 2 minutes, or until the spinach is just wilted.

Remove from the heat and allow to cool, then process in a food processor to form a puree.

Return the pureed spinach mixture to the pan. Add the tofu carefully to avoid breaking it up, and stir through until coated. Heat gently over a low heat until hot, then serve.

As a child, I loved helping my extended family shell the peas to make this simple, fresh and delicious recipe. Many winter afternoons in Delhi were spent sitting in the warmth of the sun with a huge stack of fresh peas, discussing the really important issues of life, such as what should accompany the green peas at dinner! To do justice to the delicate flavours of this dish, you should really use fresh peas. You can use frozen peas, but the results will not be as good. Also, eat it on its own so you can taste every element.

हरी मटर अदरक और नीबू के साथ

GREEN PEAS WITH GINGER AND LEMON

PREPARATION TIME
10 minutes

COOKING TIME
10 minutes

SERVES
4

310 g (11 oz) shelled fresh or frozen peas

15 g (½ oz) vegan ghee or vegan butter

1 green chilli

1 teaspoon ginger paste (page 25)

½ teaspoon sugar

1 tablespoon lemon juice

½–1 teaspoon salt, or to taste

Cook the peas in a large saucepan of boiling salted water over a high heat for 2–3 minutes, or until just tender. Drain and rinse under cold water.

Heat the ghee or butter in a large frying pan over a medium heat. Sauté the chilli and ginger paste, stirring continuously, for about 30 seconds. Stir in the peas and sugar and cook, stirring occasionally, for 2–4 minutes, or until heated through and the sugar has dissolved.

Quickly toss the lemon juice and salt through the peas, then serve.

In this North Indian delicacy, roasted eggplant (aubergine) is the star. There are many varieties of eggplant, but this recipe is best made with the medium-sized round or long purple varieties. For the best flavour and texture, buy eggplants when they are in season and opt for the smaller, seedless ones that feel heavy for their size. Enjoy this dish hot, with Chapattis (page 131) or Parathas (page 134).

PREPARATION TIME
10 minutes

COOKING TIME
25 minutes

SERVES
4

ढुंगरी बैंगन भरता
SMOKY EGGPLANT BHURTA

2 eggplants (aubergines)
1½ tablespoons vegetable or sunflower oil
1 small onion, chopped
1 teaspoon ginger paste (page 25)
1 teaspoon garlic paste (page 25)
2 large tomatoes, chopped
2 green chillies, chopped
½ teaspoon turmeric
large handful coriander (cilantro) leaves, chopped
½–1 teaspoon salt, or to taste

Cook the eggplants whole in a heavy-based frying pan or chargrill pan over a medium heat, or under the grill (broiler), for about 20 minutes, or until soft and the skin is charred. Turn only once or twice during cooking. Allow to cool, then cut in half. Scoop out the flesh with a spoon, chop roughly and reserve. Discard the skin.

Heat the oil in a frying pan over a medium heat. Sauté the onion, stirring occasionally, for 5 minutes, or until translucent. Add the ginger and garlic pastes and cook, stirring, for about 1 minute.

Stir in the tomato, chilli and turmeric, reduce the heat to low and cook for about 5 minutes, or until the tomato has softened.

Stir in the reserved eggplant flesh, coriander and salt and cook for a further 5 minutes. Serve hot.

PREPARATION TIME
10 minutes

COOKING TIME
30 minutes

SERVES
4

---

8 ripe tomatoes

60 ml (2 fl oz/¼ cup) vegetable or sunflower oil

1 onion, chopped

1 teaspoon ginger paste (page 25)

1 teaspoon garlic paste (page 25)

1 teaspoon ground coriander

½ teaspoon turmeric

1 teaspoon chilli powder

2 tablespoons vegan plain yoghurt

½–1 teaspoon salt, or to taste

125 ml (4 fl oz/½ cup) vegan pouring (single/light) cream

¼ teaspoon freshly ground whole mace

¼ teaspoon ground cardamom

FILLING

1 teaspoon vegetable or sunflower oil

100–150 g (3½–5½ oz) mushrooms, cleaned and finely chopped

1 teaspoon finely chopped green chilli

1 teaspoon finely chopped fresh ginger

125 g (4½ oz) fresh figs or 50–75 g (1¾–2¾ oz) finely chopped dried figs

½–1 teaspoon salt, or to taste

When tomatoes are in season, this is a great dish to make for a dinner party. Indians love stuffed vegetable recipes for a vegan dish with a difference. We fill eggplant (aubergine), capsicum (pepper), zucchini (courgette), potato, okra, bitter melon (bitter gourd), and even the spaces between the stalks and florets of broccoli, with various ingredients, such as vegan cheese, sultanas (golden raisins), nuts, tamarind, dried fruit or coconut. Serve these stuffed tomatoes with just about any of the Indian breads.

ढींगरी और अंजीर से भरे टमाटर

TOMATOES FILLED WITH MUSHROOMS AND FIGS

Cut the tops off the tomatoes and discard. Scoop out the pulp, reserving this and the hollowed-out tomato shells separately.

To make the filling, heat the oil in a medium frying pan or saucepan over a medium heat. Sauté the mushrooms, chilli and ginger, stirring occasionally, for about 5 minutes. Add the figs and salt and cook, stirring occasionally, for about 10 minutes if using fresh figs, or for 6 minutes if using dried figs.

Using a spoon, fill the hollowed-out tomatoes with the filling, pressing it in firmly. Set aside.

In a large frying pan, heat the oil over a low heat. Sauté the onion, stirring occasionally, for about 5 minutes, or until golden brown. Stir in the ginger and garlic pastes and cook for 2 minutes. Add the coriander, turmeric, chilli powder, reserved tomato pulp, yoghurt and salt and stir, then cook until heated through. Stir in the cream and simmer for 2 minutes. Combine the mace and cardamom in a small bowl, then stir into the sauce.

Carefully place the stuffed tomatoes in the sauce and simmer gently over a low heat for about 20 minutes, or until they are soft. (You can cover the pan if you want to speed up the cooking time.) Serve hot.

Okra, or lady's fingers as they are known in India, is a summer vegetable, best eaten when in season, and a favourite vegetable of mine. Use only young okra and cook them uncovered to achieve a crisp – as opposed to a slimy – texture. While frozen okra is available from Indian and Middle Eastern grocery stores, it lacks the crisp texture and flavour of fresh okra. In this dish the okra is cooked with tomato and onion – *do pyaz* means 'double onion'. Serve it as an accompaniment to a main meal.

भिंडी दो प्याज़
OKRA DO PYAZ

PREPARATION TIME
10 minutes

COOKING TIME
20 minutes

SERVES
4

2 tablespoons vegetable or sunflower oil

1 teaspoon cumin seeds

1 dried whole red chilli

1 onion, sliced

250 g (9 oz) small, young okra

2 tomatoes, cut into wedges

½ teaspoon turmeric

½–1 teaspoon salt, or to taste

Heat the oil in a large wok or frying pan over a medium heat. Stir in the cumin seeds and chilli and cook until the cumin seeds start to crackle. Immediately add the onion and sauté, stirring occasionally, for about 5 minutes, or until translucent.

Add the okra, tomato and turmeric, stir to mix through, then cook, uncovered, for 15 minutes, or until the okra is soft.

Add the salt and cook for a further 2–3 minutes. (It is important to add the salt last, otherwise the okra has a tendency to become slimy.) Serve hot.

PREPARATION TIME
15 minutes

COOKING TIME
15 minutes

SERVES
4

---

80 g (2¾ oz) vegan ghee or 80 ml (3 fl oz/⅓ cup) vegetable or sunflower oil
2 tablespoons garlic paste (page 25)
4 tablespoons balti masala (page 21)
5 tomatoes, chopped
3 green chillies, chopped
2 tablespoons finely chopped fresh ginger
large handful coriander (cilantro) leaves, chopped
180 g (6½ oz) large mushrooms, cleaned and diced, or button mushrooms, cleaned
125 g (4½ oz) baby spinach, washed and drained
½–1 teaspoon salt, or to taste

Karahi-style cooking is done over a high heat for a very short time. The extreme heat leads to its characteristic flavour. A karahi is an Indian wok that is slightly deeper than a traditional Asian wok and made of a thicker metal, such as cast iron. It is used for stir-frying, deep-frying and simmering, covered, over a very low heat to preserve colour and flavour. Serve this karahi of spinach and mushrooms with Naan (page 128), Bhaturas (page 133) or Parathas (page 134).

करहै पालकौर ढींगरी

KARAHI-STYLE BABY SPINACH AND MUSHROOMS

Heat the ghee or oil in a wok or large frying pan over a high heat. Stir-fry the garlic paste for 2 minutes, or until golden brown. Add the balti masala and stir-fry for 1 minute.

Stir in the tomato and cook until it starts to bubble. Add the chilli, three-quarters of the ginger and one-third of the coriander, stir to mix well and simmer for 5 minutes.

Stir in the mushrooms and baby spinach and cook for about 3 minutes, or until tender. Season with the salt to taste and stir well.

Garnish with the remaining ginger and coriander and serve hot.

As young children, we took our regular holidays in Dehradun, in the Himalayan foothills, with my grandparents. As a special treat, my grandmother would send out for this pumpkin dish with freshly made Pooris. The sight of my grandparents' cook, Moti Singh, cycling back with the goodies swinging in a bag from the handlebars would set all of us drooling, while he pretended to be affronted that we preferred the 'bought stuff' to his home-cooked delicacies.

हलवाई का कद्दू
SPICY PUMPKIN

PREPARATION TIME
20 minutes

COOKING TIME
40 minutes

SERVES
4

- 1½ tablespoons vegetable or sunflower oil
- ¼ teaspoon fennel seeds
- ¼ teaspoon fenugreek seeds
- ¼ teaspoon black mustard seeds
- ¼ teaspoon nigella (kalonji)
- 1 dried whole red chilli
- 500 g (1 lb 2 oz) butternut pumpkin (squash), peeled and diced
- 1 tablespoon tamarind pulp (page 25)
- 2 teaspoons sugar
- 1 teaspoon ground coriander
- pinch of asafoetida
- 1 teaspoon chilli powder
- ½–1 teaspoon salt, or to taste

Heat the oil in a large saucepan over a medium heat. Add the fennel seeds, fenugreek seeds, mustard seeds, nigella, dried red chilli and pumpkin and sauté, stirring continuously to coat the pumpkin with the spices, for about 1 minute.

Stir in the tamarind pulp, sugar, coriander, asafoetida, chilli powder and salt with 250 ml (8½ fl oz/1 cup) water. Reduce the heat to low, cover and cook for about 30 minutes, or until the pumpkin is soft and starting to disintegrate. Serve hot as an accompaniment to vegetable main courses such as Green bean thoran (page 67), Corn takatak (page 68) or Okra do pyaz (page 86), or by itself with Pooris (page 132).

PREPARATION TIME
30 minutes

COOKING TIME
60 minutes

SERVES
4

- 500g (1 lb 2 oz/3 cups jackfruit pieces (fresh or tinned – see Note)
- 2 tablespoons vegetable or sunflower oil
- 3 large potatoes, peeled and halved
- 5 cloves, ground
- 4 black peppercorns, ground
- 2 tablespoons poppy seeds, finely ground
- 1 tablespoon coriander seeds, ground
- 1 tablespoon fennel seeds, ground
- 1–2 tablespoons chilli powder, to taste
- small handful coriander (cilantro) leaves, chopped, to garnish

MARINADE
- ½–2 teaspoons salt, or to taste
- 2 teaspoons turmeric
- 1 tablespoon ginger paste (page 25)
- 1 tablespoon garlic paste (page 25)

ONION AND TOMATO PASTE
- 2 tablespoons vegetable or canola oil
- 3 large onions, chopped
- 45 g (1½ oz/½ cup) shredded (grated dried) coconut
- 2 tomatoes, chopped

This is a very spicy hot red vegetable curry from Kolhapur in western India – reduce the chilli if you would like a medium-hot version. I came across this recipe when I worked in Mumbai during the 1980s. It was quite a shock to my tame North-East Indian palate – and is a winner at the Spice Kitchen with all the macho male diners. Serve with plenty of steamed basmati or other long-grain rice.

कटहल कोहलापुरी

JACKFRUIT KOLHAPURI

To make the marinade, mix together the salt, turmeric and ginger and garlic pastes in a large bowl. Add the jackfruit and stir to coat thoroughly, then cover and put in the refrigerator to marinate for 1 hour.

To make the onion and tomato paste, heat the oil in a large heavy-based saucepan over a medium heat. Sauté the onion, stirring occasionally, for about 5 minutes, or until brown. Stir in the coconut and tomato and cook for about 2 minutes. Remove from the heat and allow to cool a little, then transfer the mixture to a food processor and process to a paste. Set aside.

Heat the oil in the same saucepan over a high heat. Add the jackfruit with its marinade and the potato and stir-fry for about 8 minutes, or until well browned.

Reduce the heat to medium. Stir in the ground cloves, black peppercorns, poppy seeds, coriander seeds, fennel seeds and chilli powder, the onion and tomato paste and 250 ml (8½ fl oz/1 cup) water. Cover and cook for about 45 minutes.

Garnish with the coriander leaves and serve hot.

NOTE: If using fresh jackfruit, be sure to wear gloves or coat your hands with oil before handling it, as it secretes a sticky juice that makes it very difficult to work with.

PREPARATION TIME
20 minutes

COOKING TIME
30 minutes

SERVES
4

2 tablespoons coconut oil
1 onion, chopped
90 g (½ cup) turnip or yam, diced
60 g (½ cup) snake beans, in large pieces
60 g (½ cup) drumsticks (moringa)
60 g (½ cup) white radish (daikon), diced
90g (½ cup) potato or sweet potato, diced
½ cup carrot, diced
1 tablespoon ground cumin
1 teaspoon turmeric
1 tablespoon ginger paste (page 25)
1 tablespoon garlic paste (page 25)
1 tablespoon poppy seeds, ground
2.5 cm (1 in) cinnamon stick
½ teaspoon black peppercorns
3–4 green chillies, slit to just below the stalk area, top and seeds left intact
1 tomato, chopped
250 ml (8½ fl oz/1 cup) coconut milk
½–1 teaspoon salt, or to taste

Vegetable moilee is a really easy, delicate recipe from Kerala, with poppy seeds and coconut imparting a lovely creaminess to the dish. Serve simply with Onion uthappams (page 46) or, for a truly authentic feel, on a banana leaf with just-cooked fluffy white rice and Green bean thoran (page 67) – the perfect foils for the moilee's subtle flavours.

सब्ज़ी की मोली

VEGETABLE MOILEE

Heat the oil in a large heavy-based saucepan over a medium heat. Sauté the onion, stirring occasionally, for about 5 minutes, or until translucent.

Stir in the vegetables, cumin, turmeric, ginger and garlic pastes, poppy seeds, cinnamon, peppercorns, chilli, tomato, coconut milk and salt. Reduce the heat to low, cover and simmer for about 30 minutes, or until the vegetables are tender. Serve hot.

PREPARATION TIME
20 minutes

COOKING TIME
20 minutes

SERVES
4

375g (13 oz/3 cups) cauliflower, diced (include some stalks and leaves)
1 teaspoon turmeric
½–1 teaspoon salt, or to taste
2 tablespoons vegetable or sunflower oil
1 onion, sliced
1 tablespoon ginger paste (page 25)
1 tablespoon garlic paste (page 25)
2 green chillies
1 tablespoon ground coriander
1 teaspoon chilli powder
6 ripe tomatoes, diced, or 600 g (1.5 x 400 g tins) tinned diced tomatoes, drained
2 yellow, red or green capsicums (peppers), diced
coriander (cilantro) leaves to garnish

फूलगोभी मसाला
CAULIFLOWER MASALA

This simple North Indian cauliflower dish is deliciously different from the coconut curries of South and West India, and is very popular in restaurants because it is quite easy to make and it does not need a lot of spices. The tomato–capsicum combination is delectable and appeals to a wide range of tastebuds. Serve with steamed basmati or other long-grain rice and Naan (page 128).

Put the cauliflower in a large bowl. Sprinkle over the turmeric and salt and toss to thoroughly coat the cauliflower. Set aside.

Heat the oil in a large frying pan. Sauté the onion over a medium heat, stirring occasionally, for 6–8 minutes, or until golden brown. Stir in the ginger and garlic pastes and the green chillies and cook for 2 minutes.

Add the ground coriander and chilli powder and cook, stirring, for about 1 minute, or until the spices release their aroma. Add the tomato and capsicum and cook over a medium heat, stirring occasionally, for about 4 minutes, or until the tomato has softened.

Add the cauliflower and cook, covered, until the cauliflower is just soft and firm to the bite – about 10 minutes. Garnish with the coriander leaves and serve hot.

The good folk of Kolkata have a reputation for arguing about everything, and food is no exception. A unanimous decision on the best vegetable curry could never be made, although if you like mustard, this recipe would be a strong contender. You can substitute okra, green beans, drumsticks (moringa) or ridge gourd for the broccoli. This recipe is usually baked, but it can also be steamed. (If steaming, reduce the cooking time by half.) Serve it with steamed basmati rice.

PREPARATION TIME
10 minutes

COOKING TIME
20 minutes

SERVES
4

सरसो ब्रोकोली
BAKED MUSTARD BROCCOLI

500 g (1 lb 2 oz) broccoli, cut into large florets

MUSTARD PASTE

½ teaspoon turmeric

1 tablespoon yellow mustard seeds, coarsely crushed

1 tablespoon black mustard seeds, coarsely crushed

1 teaspoon hot English mustard

2 tablespoons mustard oil

250 ml (8½ fl oz/1 cup) coconut milk

4 green chillies

½–1 teaspoon salt, or to taste

Preheat the oven to 170°C (340°F).

To make the mustard paste, mix together the turmeric, yellow and black mustard seeds, hot English mustard, mustard oil, coconut milk, chillies and salt in a large bowl. Add the broccoli florets to the bowl and stir to coat thoroughly with the mustard paste.

Put the broccoli with the paste in a shallow baking dish with a lid. Cover tightly and cook in the oven for about 15 minutes. Serve hot.

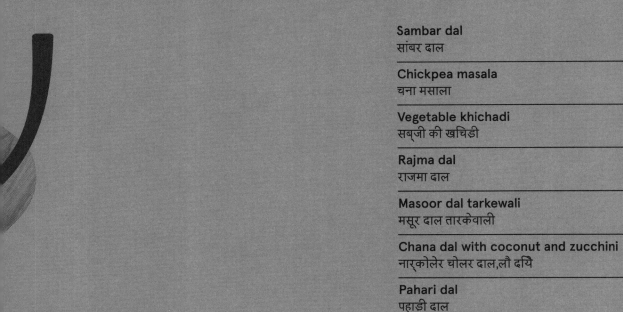

Sambar dal सांबर दाल	100
Chickpea masala चना मसाला	103
Vegetable khichadi सब्जी की खिचडी	104
Rajma dal राजमा दाल	105
Masoor dal tarkewali मसूर दाल तारकेवाली	107
Chana dal with coconut and zucchini नार्कोलेर चोलर दाल, लौ दिये	109
Pahari dal पहाडी दाल	110
Spinach kadhi पालक कढी	111

Open the doors of the pantry in an Indian home and you're likely to find at least ten different kinds of pulses of all colours, some with their skin on and others without it, some split, and still others made into flour. These are eaten in many delicious guises throughout the day. Whether it is a dosa or uthappam at breakfast, a simple dal with rice or roti at lunch, or a slightly more extravagant preparation such as Mushroom and chickpea pulao (page 121) at dinner, pulses are sure to feature. In the south, no meal is complete without a sambar (see Sambar dal, page 100) or a soup-like rasam (try Mulligatawny soup, page 42).

The most commonly used pulses in India are masoor dal (split red lentils); yellow or green mung beans (green when whole, yellow when split); toor or arhar dal (yellow split peas, often called 'pigeon peas' in English); urad dal (black lentils, or white when their black skin is removed); chana dal (split, dehusked chickpeas); and, of course, the chickpea itself. Other pulses, such as dried red kidney beans, are also popular. Most pulses with skin on, including chickpeas and dried beans, need to be soaked for at least six hours in cold water before cooking; those with their skin removed can be cooked straight away and usually take thirty minutes to one hour to soften. For use in salads and curries, pulses are often sprouted, and for pancake-like recipes such as fritters and dumplings, they are fermented.

Nutritionally, pulses are an excellent source of protein, which is particularly important for vegans, who are not obtaining protein from meat. They are also full of fibre, as well as vitamins and minerals such as iron and folate. They have no cholesterol and their low glycaemic index helps to regulate insulin and blood sugar.

While pulses may not be flavour-packed in themselves, they are far from boring when teamed with Indian spices. (Many spices, such as asafoetida and ginger, also combat the flatulence for which pulses are known and feared.) In short, pulses are the ultimate comfort food, adored by all demographics and unquestionably a vegan mainstay.

A sambar is a South Indian lentil preparation that usually includes vegetables and is flavoured with tamarind. Almost any vegetable can be used in a sambar, and the tamarind provides tartness and preserves the vitamins of the cooked vegetables. Sambars are eaten with steamed basmati rice or served with dishes such as Cabbage bondas (page 49) or Upma (page 56).

PREPARATION TIME
10 minutes

COOKING TIME
40 minutes

SERVES
4

सांबर दाल
SAMBAR DAL

Put the lentils, turmeric and 750 ml (25½ fl oz/3 cups) water in a large saucepan over a medium heat. Bring to a boil and cook, uncovered, for about 30 minutes, or until the lentils are soft. (Whole red lentils will take a little longer to cook than the split variety.)

Meanwhile, to make the sambar paste, grind the yellow split peas using a mortar and pestle or an electric spice grinder. Transfer to a small bowl and mix with the fenugreek, chilli powder, cumin, coriander, coconut and tamarind pulp to form a paste

When the lentils are cooked, stir in the sambar paste, eggplant, cauliflower, green beans and tomato and cook over a medium heat for 15 minutes. Add the salt to taste.

About 5 minutes before the sambar is ready, make the tempering. Heat the ghee or butter in a small frying pan over a high heat. Add the mustard, cumin and fenugreek seeds, dried chillies and curry leaves and heat until they begin to crackle. Immediately add the onion and sauté, stirring occasionally, for about 5 minutes, or until golden brown.

Pour the tempering over the sambar, garnish with chopped coriander leaves if desired, and serve.

125 g (4½ oz/½ cup) split red lentils (masoor dal) or whole red lentils, washed and drained

1 teaspoon turmeric

½ small eggplant (aubergine), diced

¼ small cauliflower, divided into small florets

12 green beans, trimmed and diced

1 large tomato, chopped

½–1 teaspoon salt, or to taste

chopped coriander (cilantro) leaves to garnish, if desired

SAMBAR PASTE

2 tablespoons yellow split peas

¼ teaspoon ground fenugreek

1 teaspoon chilli powder

1 teaspoon ground cumin

2 tablespoons ground coriander

3 tablespoons shredded (grated dried) coconut

1 tablespoon tamarind pulp (page 25)

TEMPERING

30 g (1 oz) vegan ghee or salted vegan butter

½ teaspoon black mustard seeds

1 teaspoon cumin seeds

¼ teaspoon fenugreek seeds

2 whole dried red chillies

20 curry leaves

1 small onion, chopped

PREPARATION TIME
20 minutes (plus soaking time)

COOKING TIME
120 minutes

SERVES
4

---

200 g (7 oz) dried chickpeas or 1 x 400 g (14 oz) tin chickpeas, rinsed and drained
1 black tea bag (see Note)
½–1 teaspoon salt, or to taste
1½ tablespoons vegetable or sunflower oil
1 small onion, chopped
1 tablespoon crushed garlic
1 tablespoon finely shredded fresh ginger
2 green chillies, slit to just below the stalk area, top and seeds left intact
1 tomato, chopped
1 tablespoon ground coriander
1 tablespoon ground cumin
pinch of turmeric
1 teaspoon chilli powder
1 teaspoon ground amchur
½ teaspoon garam masala (page 20)
small handful chopped coriander (cilantro) leaves
lemon wedges to garnish
green chillies to garnish
red (Spanish) onion quarters to garnish
julienned fresh ginger to garnish

A Delhi and Punjabi street-food favourite, you can find chickpea masala and bhaturas – fluffy, fried breads – at almost every street cafe and cart. The masala is arranged in a mouth-watering mound, and scattered with lemon wedges, whole green chillies, slices of red (Spanish) onion and pieces of tomato. I might never have got through university without my regular visit to the chickpea and bhatura vendor, where there was always an impatient queue. Serve this masala with Bhaturas (page 133) for brunch or lunch, or with other dishes as part of an Indian meal.

चना मसाला

CHICKPEA MASALA

If using dried chickpeas, soak overnight in a bowl of cold water. Drain, then put in a large saucepan with the tea bag, salt and 1.5 litres (51 fl oz/6 cups) fresh water. Cover, bring to a boil, then reduce the heat and cook over a medium heat for 1–2 hours, or until tender. Skim off the residue as it rises to the surface during cooking. Drain the cooked chickpeas, reserving 250 ml (8½ fl oz/1 cup) of the cooking liquid.

Heat the oil in a large frying pan over a medium heat. Sauté the onion, stirring occasionally, for about 7 minutes, or until golden brown.

Stir in the garlic, ginger and green chilli and sauté, stirring occasionally, for 2 minutes. Add the tomato, ground coriander and cumin, turmeric, chilli powder and amchur and stir to combine, then cook for 2–3 minutes.

Stir in the cooked chickpeas and their reserved cooking liquid, or the drained tinned chickpeas and 250 ml (8½ fl oz/1 cup) water. Continue cooking, uncovered, for 30 minutes. When the liquid is almost absorbed, finish the dish by sprinkling in the garam masala and chopped coriander and stirring through.

Serve garnished with lemon wedges, green chillies, onion quarters and julienned ginger.

NOTE: The tea bag gives this dish its traditional dark colour and also a very faint tea flavour. Using tinned chickpeas omits this step, but you will still obtain a good result.

Vegetable khichadi originated as a peasant dish in ancient India. It can be cooked dry or quite wet, with a variety of vegetables. For me, this is the best comfort food, guaranteed to produce a warm fuzzy feeling. It is usually served for lunch with a dry vegetable curry such as Vegetable Chakka (page 77) and a sweet or spicy chutney (page 154). Or, the crispness of Banana chilli and potato pakoras (page 51) contrasts delectably with the lovely mushiness of the khichadi.

PREPARATION TIME
20 minutes

COOKING TIME
40 minutes

SERVES
4

सब्ज़ी की खिचड़ी

VEGETABLE KHICHADI

Heat the ghee or oil in a large heavy-based saucepan with a tight-fitting lid over a medium heat. Stir in the bay leaves, cinnamon, green and black cardamom pods, cloves and peppercorns and cook for 5 seconds. Immediately add the onion and sauté, stirring occasionally, for about 5 minutes, or until golden brown.

Add the rice and mung dal or masoor dal, the mixed vegetables of your choice, 1 litre (34 fl oz/4 cups) boiling water (see Note) and the salt and stir to mix through. Cover and bring to a boil, then reduce the heat to low and simmer for 30–40 minutes, or until the rice and dal are cooked. Serve hot.

NOTE: The consistency of khichadi may be fairly moist, like this recipe, or it may be dry. If you prefer a drier version, reduce the amount of boiling water you add with the rice, dried beans and vegetables to 625 ml (21 fl oz/2½ cups).

---

30 g (1 oz) vegan ghee or 2 tablespoons vegetable or sunflower oil

3 bay leaves

1 cm (½ in) cinnamon stick

3 green cardamom pods

2 black cardamom pods

4 cloves

4 black peppercorns

1 large onion, sliced

135 g (5 oz/⅔ cup) basmati rice or other long-grain rice, washed and drained

100 g (3½ oz) mung dal (split dried mung beans) or masoor dal (split red lentils), washed and drained

250 g (9 oz) diced mixed seasonal vegetables, choosing 2–3 of the following:
- 4 small cauliflower florets
- 4 small new potatoes, scrubbed
- 1 sweet potato, peeled
- 12 green beans, trimmed
- 1 carrot, peeled
- 100 g (3½ oz) pumpkin (winter squash), peeled

½–1 teaspoon salt, or to taste

PREPARATION TIME
20 minutes (plus soaking time)

COOKING TIME
150 minutes

SERVES
4

---

225 g (8 oz) dried or 600 g (1 lb 5 oz) tinned red kidney beans

60 g (2 oz) vegan ghee, or 60 ml (2 fl oz/¼ cup) vegetable or sunflower oil (see Note)

1 teaspoon cumin seeds

1 teaspoon chilli powder

1 tablespoon julienned fresh ginger

1 large onion, sliced

60 g (2 oz/¼ cup) tomato paste (concentrated puree) or 2 vine-ripened tomatoes, chopped

---

Punjab is India's agricultural bowl. Punjabi cuisine abounds with nourishing and satisfying country-style recipes that use locally grown ingredients, such as chickpeas and red kidney beans, wheat and corn flours. Rajma dal is a Punjabi favourite – this simple dish is satisfying and healthy, full of fibre and protein. You may not have to work a 12-hour day on a farm, but you will certainly get enough energy from this dish, served with rice, to face the world for many hours to come.

राजमा दाल

RAJMA DAL

If using dried red kidney beans, soak overnight in a bowl of cold salted water. Drain, then put in a medium saucepan with 1.5 litres (51 fl oz/6 cups) fresh water. Bring to a boil, then reduce the heat to medium and cook, uncovered, skimming off the residue as it rises to the surface, for about 2½ hours, or until the beans are really tender – they should break up easily when pressed between your thumb and forefinger. Drain the cooked kidney beans, reserving 375 ml (12½ fl oz/1½ cups) of the cooking liquid. Alternatively, if you are using tinned red kidney beans, rinse them well in cold water and drain.

Heat the ghee or oil over a medium heat in a large frying pan. Add the cumin seeds, chilli powder and ginger and heat until they begin to crackle. Add the onion and sauté, stirring occasionally, for about 8 minutes, or until golden brown.

Stir in the tomato paste or chopped tomato with 125 ml (4 fl oz/½ cup) water and simmer gently over a low heat for 10 minutes. Add the cooked kidney beans with the reserved cooking liquid, or the drained tinned kidney beans along with 250 ml (8½ oz/1 cup) water, and simmer for a further 20 minutes. Serve hot.

NOTE: Vegan ghee really is preferable for this recipe. You can replace it with oil, but the final flavour will not be as rich.

PREPARATION TIME
10 minutes

COOKING TIME
50 minutes

SERVES
4

250 g (9 oz/1 cup) split red lentils (masoor dal) or whole red lentils, washed and drained
1 teaspoon chopped fresh ginger
1 teaspoon chopped garlic
½ small onion, sliced
1 teaspoon turmeric
½–1 teaspoon salt, or to taste
TEMPERING
60 g (2 oz) vegan ghee or vegan butter
2 teaspoons cumin seeds
1 onion, sliced
1 whole dried red chilli
pinch of chilli powder
2 tablespoons chopped coriander (cilantro) leaves

Lentils are an important part of the Indian meal. They are a great leveller and comfort food for both the street dweller and the penthouse millionaire. The split red lentils (masoor dal) used in this recipe are similar to the whole red lentils found in supermarkets – they do not need soaking and are easy to cook. They are also very easy to digest. Eat with steamed rice or homemade Indian bread such as Chapattis (page 131), accompanied by vegetable dishes.

मसूर दाल तारकेवाली

MASOOR DAL TARKEWALI

Put the lentils, ginger, garlic, onion and turmeric, along with 750 ml (25½ fl oz/3 cups) water in a large saucepan and stir to combine. Cook, uncovered, over a medium heat for about 45 minutes, or until the lentils are well cooked and disintegrating to form a puree. (Whole red lentils will take a little longer to cook than the split variety.) Stir in the salt.

To make the tempering, heat the ghee or butter in a small frying pan over a high heat. Cook the cumin seeds, onion, dried red chilli and chilli powder, stirring occasionally, for 6–8 minutes, or until the onion is golden brown. Stir in the coriander and cook for 1 minute.

Pour the tempering over the cooked dal and serve immediately.

PREPARATION TIME
15 minutes

COOKING TIME
90 minutes

SERVES
4

---

2 tablespoons mustard oil
2 cassia or bay leaves
5 cm (2 in) cinnamon stick
2 black peppercorns
2 cloves
2 green cardamom pods
1 teaspoon finely chopped fresh ginger
2 green chillies, slit
1 small onion, sliced
220 g (8 oz/1 cup) chana dal, washed and drained
1 teaspoon turmeric
¼ cup fresh coconut, diced or shredded
2 zucchini (courgettes), diced
1 tablespoon sugar
1 teaspoon salt, or to taste

Chana dal is the split chickpea similar to the yellow split pea but nuttier in flavour. It is easy to cook; no soaking is required, though pressure cooking is recommended to save some time. High in protein, it is the vegan's best friend because of its versatility (it can be used in curries, soups, vegan patties, kababs and koftas). In this recipe, it is combined with finely diced or shredded fresh coconut and zucchini. Enjoy with Pooris (page 132) or Parathas (page 134).

नার্কোলের চোলর দাল,লৌ দযি

CHANA DAL WITH COCONUT AND ZUCCHINI

In a heavy-based saucepan or a pressure cooker, heat the mustard oil until smoking. Add the cassia or bay leaves, cinnamon, pepper, cloves, cardamom pods, ginger and green chilli. Cook, stirring, for 5–10 seconds. Next, add the onion and sauté until golden brown. Now stir in the chana dal with 1 litre (34 fl oz/4 cups) of water and the turmeric.

Cook for 20 minutes in a pressure cooker or simmer for about an hour on the stovetop, until the dal is soft but not mushy. Add the coconut and cook for another 10 minutes before adding the zucchini, sugar and salt. Simmer for a further 5 minutes and serve hot.

This is a unique and unusual recipe from the Himalayan foothills. Split black lentils (urad dal), which are readily available in Indian grocery stores, are roasted and ground coarsely before use. Atta flour is used to thicken the dal, but if you'd prefer a gluten-free version, you can use besan (chickpea flour) instead. Rich in nutrients, this dal is a mainstay for the hill dwellers, where many fresh ingredients are more difficult to access. Even though the ingredients list might look relatively long, this is a very quick recipe because once the dal has been ground, it does not require much cooking time.

This dal is normally cooked on a wood fire, giving it a beautifully smoky flavour. To replicate this flavour, you can use the *dhungar* method (see page 28). Serve with Black peppercorn and cumin rice (page 118), Crispy straw potatoes (page 127) or Chapattis (page 131).

पहाड़ी दाल

PAHARI DAL

PREPARATION TIME
30 minutes

COOKING TIME
20 minutes

SERVES
4

185 g (6½ oz/¾ cup) split black lentils (urad dal)

2 tablespoons mustard oil

2 whole dried red chillies

½ teaspoon black mustard seeds

1 teaspoon ginger paste (page 25)

1 tablespoon garlic paste (page 25)

1 teaspoon crushed black peppercorns

½ teaspoon asafoetida

1 tablespoon atta flour

½ teaspoon cumin powder

½ teaspoon coriander powder

1 teaspoon turmeric

1 teaspoon salt, or to taste

Dry-roast the lentils in a heavy-based frying pan. Cool and crush coarsely in a spice grinder. Keep aside.

In a large saucepan, heat mustard oil until smoking. Add the dried chillies and mustard seeds, then the ginger and garlic pastes, and the crushed black peppercorns. Mix in the asafoetida, then stir in the lentils and sauté for 2 minutes. Add the atta flour, pour in 3 cups of water and turn the heat to low. Stir in the cumin, coriander and turmeric. The dal should thicken in 5–7 minutes.

Season with salt and adjust the consistency with a little water if required. Serve hot.

PREPARATION TIME
15 minutes

COOKING TIME
30 minutes

SERVES
4

Kadhi is a great substitute for dal and is often eaten with steamed rice. The most popular version of kadhi is made with besan (chickpea flour) dumplings. This recipe uses spinach and is a delicious speedy alternative. Use white radish (daikon) or mustard greens instead, if you prefer vegetables with a slightly bitter flavour.

| 110 g (4 oz/1 cup) besan (chickpea flour) |
| 125 g (4½ oz/½ cup) vegan plain yoghurt |
| 1 teaspoon turmeric |
| 30 g (1 oz) vegan ghee or 1½ tablespoons mustard oil |
| 1 small onion, sliced |
| 1 teaspoon cumin seeds |
| 2 dried whole red chillies |
| pinch of asafoetida |
| ½–1 teaspoon salt, to taste |
| 50 g (1¾ oz) English spinach, washed, drained and finely chopped |
| 1 tablespoon chopped mint leaves |

पालक कढ़ी

SPINACH KADHI

In a large bowl mix together the besan, yoghurt, turmeric and 500 ml (17 fl oz/2 cups) water to make a smooth paste.

Heat the ghee or oil in a medium saucepan over a medium heat. Sauté the onion, stirring occasionally, for about 5 minutes, or until golden brown. Add the cumin seeds, chillies and asafoetida and stir to mix well. Add the besan paste, salt and another 500 ml (17 fl oz/2 cups) water to obtain a thin sauce-like consistency.

Cook, stirring continuously, for about 30 minutes, or until the kadhi thickens. The final consistency should be like a thick soup. Add the spinach and mint and briefly bring to a boil. Remove from the heat and serve immediately.

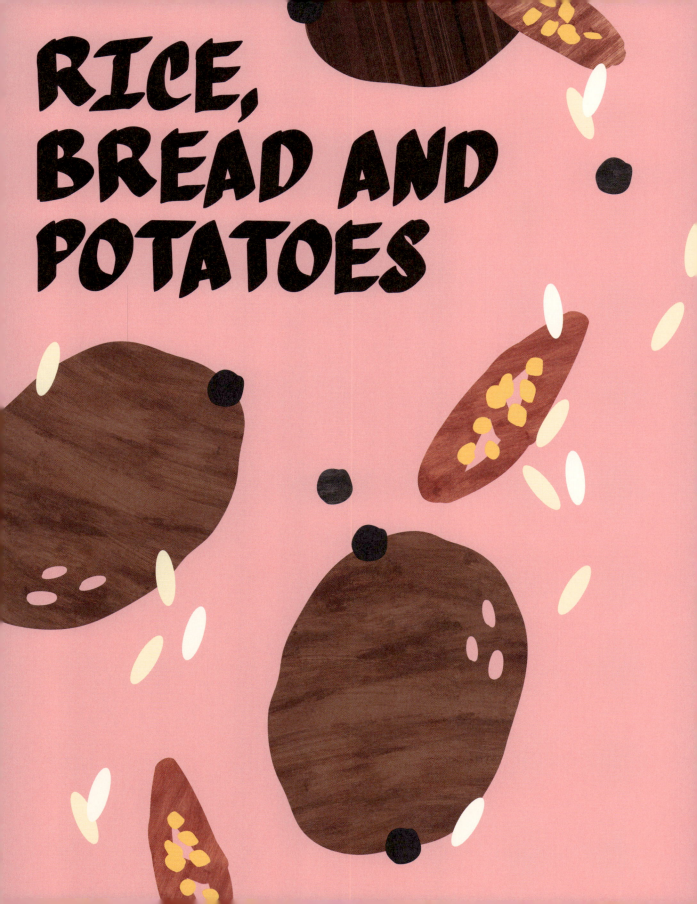

Lemon rice नींबू चावल	117
Black peppercorn and cumin rice काली मिर्च और जीरा चावल	118
Pulao rice पुलाव चावल	120
Mushroom and chickpea pulao ढींगरी और चने का पुलाव	121
Tomato pulao rice टमाटर पुलाव चावल	122
Potatoes with cumin seeds जीरा के साथ आलू	124
Poppy seed potatoes आलू पोस्टो खसखस आलू	126
Crispy straw potatoes कुरकुरा भूसा आलू	127
Naan नान	128
Chapattis चपाती	131
Pooris पूरी	132
Bhaturas भटूरे	133
Parathas परांठे	134
Green mung roti हरी मूंग दाल की रोटी	136
Missie roti मिस्सी रोटी	137

The most common side dish served with an Indian meal is rice, whether steamed or fried, prepared simply or elaborately. Many varieties are consumed. In the north, the most well known is basmati; its lovely slender grains release less starch than the shorter varieties, making it light and fluffy when cooked.

While rice is a staple in much of the country, a variety of breads are also eaten with meals. For breakfast, pooris and parathas are favourites, often stuffed with vegetables and eaten on their own or with plain yoghurt.

The potato, commonly found in western menus as an alternative to rice or bread, plays its own starring role in India, where rice, bread and potato are frequently all served in a single meal. In this chapter, I have included some of the simpler potato recipes, which are generally served as accompaniments or sides.

When buying rice, it's a good idea to check its age (this information is generally available on the packet). Try to buy already-aged rice, which has a creamier colour and is usually more expensive. Aged rice will cook without getting gluggy or breaking up, and has a better flavour. New crops or just-harvested rice should be stored for up to five years to allow the flavours to develop and the starch content to reduce.

Breads make the perfect accompaniment to aromatic dry and wet curries, and are particularly good for mopping up unctuous sauces. In India, plain (all-purpose) flour, wholemeal atta flour, besan (chickpea flour) and maize flour are used to make leavened bread, such as naan and bhaturas, and unleavened bread, such as pooris, chapattis and parathas. (As the demand for gluten-free flours has increased, other peasant-style flours, such as finger millet and ragi flour, have become more mainstream.) Kids will love butter and jam chapatti rolls: simply spread butter and jam on a chapatti and roll it up like a pancake, or try adding jaggery instead of jam.

RICE, BREAD AND POTATOES

PREPARATION TIME
25 minutes

COOKING TIME
15 minutes

SERVES
4

---

1 teaspoon fenugreek seeds

1 tablespoon split white lentils (white urad dal), washed and drained (see Notes)

1 teaspoon turmeric

225 g (8 oz) cooked basmati rice or other long-grain rice, at room temperature (see Notes)

juice of 2 lemons

2 tablespoons vegetable or sunflower oil

30 g (1 oz) raw cashew nuts

30 g (1 oz) raw peanuts

½–1 teaspoon salt, or to taste

TEMPERING

20 curry leaves

½ teaspoon black mustard seeds

pinch of asafoetida

1 tablespoon yellow split peas, washed and drained

2 red chillies

Rice recipes that use already-cooked rice are popular in South India, and lemon rice is considered a delicacy there. It is a lovely way to use up leftover rice. If freshly cooked, the rice should be at room temperature – stirring the hot tempering through will heat it up. You can serve it hot on a banana leaf with an assortment of curries or just with yoghurt and pickle. It is also great as a warm or cold salad.

नीबू चावल

LEMON RICE

Heat the fenugreek seeds and split white lentils in a heavy-based frying pan over a medium heat for 1 minute. Remove from heat and allow to cool, then grind finely with the turmeric using a mortar and pestle or an electric spice grinder.

Put the cooked rice in a large bowl and stir through the ground lentil mixture and lemon juice.

Heat the oil over a medium heat in the frying pan. Cook the cashew nuts and peanuts, stirring continuously, for about 2 minutes, or until golden brown. Remove the nuts from the pan, drain on kitchen towels and set aside.

Using the oil in the frying pan, make the tempering: add the curry leaves, mustard seeds, asafoetida, yellow split peas and chillies to the pan and cook, stirring continuously, for 2 minutes, or until the mixture is brown.

Pour the tempering over the rice, add the salt and stir to mix thoroughly.

Garnish with the reserved nuts and serve.

NOTES: In South Indian cooking, a contrast in texture is often provided by adding lentils and pulses to cooked vegetables. They are not necessarily cooked until soft. Instead, as with the yellow split peas in this recipe, they are washed and drained, then quickly fried in hot oil or vegan ghee for 1–2 minutes. This gives them a crunchy texture, and as they are fully cooked, they are fine to eat.

You need 100 g (3½ oz) of uncooked rice to yield 225 g (8 oz) of cooked rice.

PREPARATION TIME
5 minutes

COOKING TIME
15 minutes

SERVES
4

---

60 g (2 oz) vegan ghee, or 60 ml (2 fl oz/¼ cup) vegetable or sunflower oil

1 teaspoon black peppercorns

1 teaspoon cumin seeds

280 g (10 oz/1½ cups) cooked basmati rice or other long-grain rice (see Note)

½–1 teaspoon salt, or to taste

There is always steamed white rice left over in an Indian home. You can add all kinds of ingredients to make complex dishes, but a really good way to refresh leftover rice is with this simple recipe. It is so popular that steamed rice is often cooked specifically to make this dish in its own right. You can serve it as part of an Indian meal, but it is also delicious with a stew or casserole.

काली मिर्च और जीरा चावल

BLACK PEPPERCORN AND CUMIN RICE

Heat the ghee or oil in a wok or large frying pan over a medium heat. Add the peppercorns and cumin seeds and cook, stirring occasionally, for about 1 minute.

Stir in the cooked rice and salt and heat through, stirring continuously to break up any lumps of rice, for about 4 minutes. Serve hot.

NOTE: You need 125 g (4½ oz) of uncooked rice to yield 280 g (10 oz/1½ cups) of cooked rice.

Pulao, from the Persian word *pilaf,* is the beautiful, fragrant, separated rice that is cooked with subtle spices and eaten throughout India. It is the most popular rice accompaniment to serve at an Indian banquet. You can cook pulao rice on the stovetop or in the oven, and vegetables such as potatoes or peas can be added, too. Serve it with all kinds of vegan curries.

PREPARATION TIME
5 minutes

COOKING TIME
30 minutes

SERVES
4

पुलाव चावल

PULAO RICE

60 g (2 oz) vegan ghee, or 60 ml (2 fl oz/¼ cup) vegetable or sunflower oil

4 green cardamom pods

3 cloves

2.5 cm (1 in) cinnamon stick

200 g (7 oz/1 cup) basmati rice or other long-grain rice, washed and drained (see Note)

½–1 teaspoon salt, or to taste

If using the oven for the final stage of cooking the rice, preheat it to 200°C (400°F).

Heat the ghee or oil in a flameproof casserole dish over a medium heat on the stovetop.

Add the cardamom pods, cloves, cinnamon and rice and stir to mix through and coat every rice grain with the ghee or oil. Pour in 375 ml (12½ fl oz/1½ cups) hot water, then add the salt and stir. Bring to a boil.

Reduce the heat to low, cover and cook the rice on the stovetop for about 20 minutes. Do not uncover or stir to ensure that the rice cooks evenly and does not break up. Remove from the heat and rest, still covered, for 10 minutes before serving. (This allows the rice grains to plump up to their maximum length.)

Alternatively, cover the dish with foil once it has come to a boil, then put in the oven and cook for about 25 minutes. Remove the dish from the oven but do not remove the foil, and rest the rice for 10 minutes before serving.

NOTE: To steam rice successfully, you must add the correct amount of water in proportion to the rice. For every 200 g (7 oz/1 cup) of rice, add 375 ml (12½ fl oz/ 1½ cups) water.

VARIATION: To re-create the yellow rice often found in Indian restaurants and takeaways, follow this recipe but add a pinch of turmeric after you've added the hot water.

PREPARATION TIME
20 minutes

COOKING TIME
40 minutes

SERVES
4

- 60 g (2 oz) vegan ghee or 60 ml (2 fl oz/¼ cup) vegetable or sunflower oil
- 2 green chillies
- 1 teaspoon whole mace
- 7 cloves
- 7 green cardamom pods
- 1 teaspoon black cumin seeds
- 1 small onion, sliced
- 200 g (7 oz/1 cup) basmati rice or other long-grain rice, washed and drained
- 4 large mushrooms, cleaned and diced
- 1 large tomato, diced
- 60 g (2 oz/¼ cup) vegan plain yoghurt
- 1 tablespoon chopped coriander (cilantro) leaves
- 1 tablespoon chopped mint leaves
- 100 g (3½ oz) dried chickpeas, cooked, or 160 g (5½ oz) tinned chickpeas, rinsed and drained (see Note)
- ½–1 teaspoon salt, or to taste
- 1 tablespoon saffron infusion (page 21)
- raw almonds to garnish
- unsalted roasted cashew nuts to garnish
- shelled pistachio nuts to garnish
- sultanas (golden raisins) to garnish

There is almost less rice in this dish – another Mughal favourite – than there are other goodies. The Mughals loved their dried fruit and nuts and missed them terribly until they succeeded in growing them in India. Of course, green chillies, cashew nuts and tomatoes were probably added to this recipe later by an inventive cook. This wonderful combination is a dish in itself. Serve this pulao with a raita (see Salads, page 138) and Eggplant chutney (page 165).

ढींगरी और चने का पुलाव

MUSHROOM AND CHICKPEA PULAO

Heat the ghee or oil in a shallow heavy-based saucepan over a medium heat. Stir in the chillies, mace, cloves, cardamom pods and black cumin seeds and cook for 5 seconds. Immediately add the onion and sauté, stirring occasionally, for about 5 minutes, or until golden brown.

Add the rice and stir until each grain is coated with the mixture. Add the mushroom, tomato, yoghurt, coriander and mint and stir to mix through.

Stir in 375 ml (12½ fl oz/1½ cups) boiling water, the chickpeas and salt. Cover and cook over a high heat until it comes to a boil. Reduce the heat to as low as possible and simmer gently for about 20 minutes, or until most of the water is absorbed and the rice is almost cooked.

Pour in the saffron infusion and stir through, then cover and continue cooking for a further 15 minutes, or until all the liquid is absorbed and the vegetables are tender.

Garnish with the almonds, cashew nuts, pistachio nuts and sultanas, and serve.

NOTE: To cook the dried chickpeas, soak overnight in a large bowl of water. Drain, then put in a large saucepan with plenty of fresh water. Cover, bring to a boil, then reduce the heat to medium and cook for 1–2 hours, until tender. Skim off the residue as it rises to the surface during the cooking process. When cooked, drain the chickpeas and use according to the recipe. If using tinned chickpeas, rinse well in cold water and drain before adding them to the rice.

Of the many, many recipes for pulao rice, this version appeared at the time of the first Portuguese settlement in India, around the sixteenth century. There were no tomatoes in India before then. Another distinctive feature of this dish is star anise, which is not commonly used in Indian cooking. A rosy blush covers this special rice dish. Serve it simply with a delicate korma.

PREPARATION TIME
20 minutes

COOKING TIME
40 minutes

SERVES
4

टमाटर पुलाव चावल

Tomato Pulao Rice

60 g (2 oz) vegan ghee or 60 ml (2 fl oz/¼ cup) vegetable or sunflower oil

2 star anise

4 cloves

2.5 cm (1 in) cinnamon stick

200 g (7 oz/1 cup) basmati rice or other long-grain rice, washed and drained

2 garlic cloves, chopped

250 g (9 oz/1 cup) tomato puree (pureed tomatoes) or 4 tomatoes, skin and seeds removed, pureed (see Note)

½–1 teaspoon salt, or to taste

1 teaspoon sugar (optional)

1 teaspoon cumin seeds, roasted and ground (page 18)

fried onions (see page 191) to garnish

Heat the ghee or oil in a shallow heavy-based saucepan over a high heat. Sauté the star anise, cloves, cinnamon and rice, stirring continuously, until the ghee or oil coats every rice grain.

Stir in the garlic and 375 ml (12½ fl oz/1½ cups) hot water. Bring to a boil, then reduce the heat to as low as possible, cover and cook for about 15 minutes, or until most of the water is absorbed.

Stir in the tomato puree. (It is important to add the tomato only at this stage, otherwise the rice may not cook evenly, as the acid in the tomato slows down the cooking process.) Add the salt and the sugar, if desired, if the tomato puree is very sour. Cover the pan again and continue cooking for about 12 minutes, or until all the liquid is absorbed and the rice is fully cooked.

Sprinkle over the cumin, garnish with the fried onions and serve hot.

NOTE: If you are using whole tomatoes to make the tomato puree, score a cross in the base of each tomato. Put in a heatproof bowl and cover with boiling water. Leave for 30 seconds, then transfer to cold water. When cool enough to handle, peel the skin away, starting from the cross. Cut the tomato in half, scoop out the seeds with a teaspoon and discard. Process the tomato flesh in a food processor to form a puree. You should have 250 g (9 oz/1 cup) of puree.

When designing the perfect menu, we often need a vegetable accompaniment that will not take away from the main event. This is just such a recipe. Delicious in its own right, it also complements many other flavours, so you can either serve it simply with Pooris (page 132) or Parathas (page 134), or make it part of an Indian meal.

PREPARATION TIME
15 minutes

COOKING TIME
25 minutes

SERVES
4

जीरा के साथ आलू
POTATOES WITH CUMIN SEEDS

15 g (½ oz) vegan ghee or 1 tablespoon vegetable or sunflower oil

1 whole dried red chilli

1 teaspoon cumin seeds

4 large potatoes, peeled and diced

1 teaspoon turmeric

½–1 teaspoon salt, or to taste

Heat the ghee or oil in a small wok or frying pan with a tight-fitting lid over a medium heat. Add the chilli and cumin seeds and heat until they begin to crackle. Immediately add the potato, turmeric, salt and 60 ml (2 fl oz/¼ cup) water and stir to mix through.

Reduce the heat to low, cover the wok or pan tightly and cook for about 20 minutes, or until the potato is soft. Serve immediately.

PREPARATION TIME
20 minutes

COOKING TIME
25 minutes

SERVES
4

---

1 tablespoon mustard oil or vegetable or sunflower oil (see Note)

1 teaspoon nigella (kalonji)

1 teaspoon chopped green chilli

1 tablespoon white poppy seeds, finely ground

4 large potatoes, peeled and diced

½ teaspoon turmeric

½–1 teaspoon salt, or to taste

This distinctive potato dish from Bengal is easy but special. Ground white poppy seeds – one of the world's most luxurious spices – are usually used in rich kormas and curries for a nutty, creamy texture and taste. In this radically different combination, white poppy seeds are teamed with the humble potato. Serve this dish as part of an Indian meal.

आलू पोस्टो खसखस आलू

POPPY SEED POTATOES

Heat the oil in a small saucepan over a high heat. If you are using mustard oil, wait until it is smoking. Reduce the heat to very low and add the nigella and green chilli, then immediately stir in the poppy seeds.

Stir in the potato, turmeric, salt and 125 ml (4 fl oz/½ cup) water. Cover and cook over a very low heat for about 20 minutes, or until the potato is soft and the water is absorbed. Serve hot.

NOTE: You can substitute vegetable or sunflower oil for the mustard oil, but the dish will have a less distinctive and authentic flavour.

PREPARATION TIME
30 minutes

COOKING TIME
30 minutes

SERVES
2 (makes 150 g/5½ oz)

Crisp-fried straw potatoes can be served as part of an Indian meal or they can be a component in another dish.

कुरकुरा भूसा आलू

CRISPY STRAW POTATOES

vegetable or sunflower oil for deep-frying

2 large potatoes, peeled and cut into matchsticks

½–1 teaspoon salt, or to taste

Heat the oil in a wok or deep-fryer to 200°C (400°F; see page 27).

Deep-fry the potato in small batches, stirring frequently with a slotted spoon, for about 8 minutes, or until golden brown and crisp. Remove from the oil with the slotted spoon and drain on kitchen towels.

Sprinkle with the salt and serve hot or at room temperature.

PREPARATION TIME
30 minutes (plus rising/resting time)

COOKING TIME
15 minutes

MAKES
4–6

---

400 g (14 oz/2½ cups) plain (all-purpose) flour

1 teaspoon salt

1 teaspoon sugar

3 teaspoons baking powder

3 tablespoons white vinegar

2 tablespoons sunflower oil

1 tablespoon nigella (kalonji)

melted vegan butter for glazing

Naan is a leavened bread, made with plain (all-purpose) wheat flour and cooked on the walls of the tandoor oven, where the temperature can reach up to 400°C (750°F). It is impossible to replicate this condition at home, but this recipe is the next best thing. Fresh naan is delightful served with any barbecued or tandoori food, kababs, kormas or rich curries.

नान

Mix together the flour, salt, sugar and baking powder in a large bowl, then make a well in the centre. Add the vinegar, oil and about 250 ml (8 ½ fl oz/1 cup) water. Knead well, adding more water if required to obtain a soft, pliable dough. Turn out onto a lightly floured work surface and knead for 10 minutes, or until the dough feels smooth and elastic. Place the dough in a clean bowl, cover with a damp cloth and set aside in a warm place to rise for 8 hours. The dough should rise by about half its size, and will have a yeasty smell and feel more pliable.

Divide the dough into 4–6 balls about 5 cm (2 in) in diameter, cover with a damp cloth and rest for 20 minutes.

Put a heavy baking tray under the grill (broiler) and, being sure to leave the grill door open, preheat the grill to high for at least 20 minutes. Alternatively, put a heavy baking tray on the top shelf or rack of the oven, close the door and preheat the oven to 200°C (400°F).

Press out each dough ball with your fingers to shape it into a triangle about 5 mm (¼ in) thick. Sprinkle with a little water, and then sprinkle over the nigella (the water helps the nigella to stick to the dough). Place on the heavy baking tray and grill under the grill or bake on the top shelf of the oven for about 2 minutes, or until brown flecks appear on the surface, then turn over and grill or bake on the top shelf for a further 40 seconds.

Brush with a little melted butter and serve immediately.

VARIATION: To make garlic naan, brush a triangle of dough with ½ teaspoon garlic paste (page 25) before cooking.

PREPARATION TIME
20 minutes

COOKING TIME
30 minutes

MAKES
4–6

---

150 g (5½ oz/1 cup) atta flour

vegan ghee to serve (optional)

This favourite home-style flat bread is made from unleavened atta flour, a finely ground wholemeal (whole-wheat) flour made from durum wheat. Traditionally, chapattis are served fresh from the kitchen one at a time and are usually pounced upon as soon as they hit the table. If you can't eat them all straight away, you can freeze them, then thaw as needed and reheat in the microwave.

चपाती

CHAPATTIS

Put the flour in a large bowl and make a well in the centre. Gradually pour in 125 ml (4 fl oz/½ cup) water while working in the flour, adding a little more water if necessary to form a soft dough. Turn out onto a lightly floured work surface and knead for 15 minutes, or until the dough is pliable and not sticky. Place the dough in a clean bowl, cover with a damp cloth and rest for 30 minutes.

Divide the dough into 4–6 balls, each about the size of a golf ball. On a lightly floured work surface, roll out each piece of dough until it is thin like a tortilla and about 18 cm (7 in) in diameter.

Heat a heavy-based frying pan over a medium heat. Dry-cook each chapatti for about 1 minute, then turn over and cook the other side for a further 40 seconds, carefully pressing down around the edges of the chapatti with a clean tea towel (dish towel) until it puffs up in the centre.

Spread with a little ghee, if desired, and serve immediately.

Commonly served as breakfast or a snack, pooris are fried in open kitchens in city cafes, or on food carts in train and bus stations. They are a traditional part of the thali meal – an array of five or six curries, presented in little bowls or on a metal plate along with rice, pickles and chutneys. Pooris are usually eaten with a simple potato or pumpkin curry, but sometimes with sweet dishes such as a rice pudding, or simply sprinkled with sugar.

POORIS

PREPARATION TIME
20 minutes

COOKING TIME
20 minutes

MAKES
10

---

150 g (5½ oz/1 cup) atta flour

pinch of salt

30 g (1 oz) vegan ghee or 2 tablespoons vegetable or sunflower oil

vegetable or sunflower oil for deep-frying

Put the flour, salt and ghee or oil in a large bowl. Gradually pour in 125 ml (4 fl oz/½ cup) water while working the ingredients together, adding a little more water if necessary to make a stiff but not sticky dough, which is not very pliable but holds together well. Turn out onto a lightly floured work surface and knead for 5 minutes, or until the dough feels smooth and holds together as one piece without sticking. Place the dough in a clean bowl, cover with a damp cloth and rest for 20 minutes.

Divide the dough into 10 balls, each about the size of a large marble. On a lightly oiled work surface, roll out each piece of dough with a rolling pin to form a small circle about 5 cm (2 in) in diameter and 1 cm (½ in) thick.

Heat the oil in a wok or deep-fryer to 200°C (400°F; see page 27). Deep-fry each poori for about 40 seconds, or until golden brown and puffed up, turning once with a slotted spoon and using the spoon to lightly press down on the poori as it puffs up. Remove from the oil and drain on kitchen towels. Serve hot.

PREPARATION TIME
20 minutes (plus rising time)

COOKING TIME
20 minutes

MAKES
4–6

---

300 g (10½ oz/2 cups) plain (all-purpose) flour

75 g (2¾ oz/½ cup) self-raising flour

1 teaspoon salt

¼ teaspoon sugar

60 g (2 oz/¼ cup) vegan plain yoghurt

30 g (1 oz) vegan ghee or 2 tablespoons vegetable or sunflower oil

vegetable or sunflower oil for deep-frying

A leavened deep-fried bread that uses plain (all-purpose) flour, the bhatura is cooked in little cafes all over Delhi and Punjab. It is a quintessential street food, sold from road carts. University students and office workers queue up for hours for bhatura and chickpeas. Everyone has a favourite vendor and the merits of each are hotly debated. Serve these with Chickpea masala (page 103).

भटूरे
BHATURAS

Mix together the plain and self-raising flours, salt and sugar, then make a well in the centre. Add the yoghurt, ghee or oil and 625 ml (21 fl oz/2½ cups) warm water and work through the dry ingredients to combine, adding a little more water if necessary. Knead for 8 minutes to form a sticky dough. Cover with a damp cloth, then set aside in a warm place to rise for at least 2 hours, or until it is pliable and stretchy.

Turn out onto a lightly floured work surface and knead the dough again for 5 minutes. Divide it into 4–6 balls about 3 cm (1¼ in) in diameter, cover with a damp cloth and rest for 10–15 minutes.

Oil the palms of your hands, then press and spread out each ball of dough with your fingers to form a circle about 10 cm (4 in) in diameter and 5 mm (¼ in) thick. Alternatively, roll out each piece of dough with a rolling pin on a lightly floured work surface.

Heat the oil in a wok or deep-fryer to 200°C (400°F; see page 27) – it is crucial that these breads are deep-fried in very hot oil.

Carefully put a round of dough in the very hot oil. Lightly press a slotted spoon down on the dough for about 5 seconds, then lift it off. (Pressing down for a few seconds at the start of the deep-frying compresses the steam inside the round of dough, and when the weight of the spoon is lifted off, the released steam causes the bhatura to gradually puff up during the cooking time.)

Deep-fry each bhatura for about 2 minutes, or until golden brown and puffed up, turning once with the slotted spoon. Remove from the oil and drain on kitchen towels. Serve hot.

Parathas – plain or wholemeal (whole-wheat) unleavened breads – are eaten for breakfast, lunch or dinner. They are also great for picnics and travel snacks. Spread a paratha with yoghurt or your favourite fruit jam, eat it simply with vegetables, or roll up a paratha 'wrap'. You can also use this recipe as the basis for making stuffed parathas (see Variation below).

PREPARATION TIME
25 minutes

COOKING TIME
30 minutes

MAKES
6–8

परांठे
PARATHAS

Mix together the flour and salt in a large bowl, then make a well in the centre. Add 2 tablespoons of the ghee and gradually pour in 190 ml (6½ fl oz/¾ cup) warm water while working the ingredients together, adding more water as necessary to make a pliable dough that does not stick to the sides of the bowl. Turn out onto a lightly floured work surface and knead for 5 minutes. Place the dough in a clean bowl, cover with a damp cloth and rest for 30 minutes.

Divide the dough into 6–8 balls, each about the size of a golf ball. Using a rolling pin, roll out each piece of dough on a lightly floured work surface to form a small circle about 5 cm (2 in) in diameter. Spread with a little ghee and fold in half to form a hemisphere, then spread with ghee and fold in half again to form a triangle with a curved edge. Dust with extra flour and roll out into a triangle that is 3 mm (⅛ in) thick.

Heat a heavy-based frying pan over a medium heat. Dry-cook each paratha on one side for about 1 minute, then spread with a little of the remaining ghee, turn over and cook the other side for 1 minute. It is cooked when light brown flecks appear on the underside. Spread the upper side with a little ghee, turn over again and cook for a further 30 seconds. Serve immediately.

VARIATION: You can make stuffed parathas with fillings such as mashed potato, grated radish or cauliflower mixed with a little salt and chilli powder. Put 1 teaspoon of filling in the middle of a 5 cm (2 in) circle of dough, then gather up the edges of the circle around the stuffing, bring the edges together and seal into little balls. Roll out into a thin circular shape, dust with atta flour and follow the cooking instructions for plain parathas.

300 g (10 oz/2 cups) atta flour, plus extra for dusting

1 teaspoon salt

125 g (4½ oz/½ cup) vegan ghee

Surprisingly, the whole green mung bean is used with atta flour to make the dough for this lovely simple flatbread. Not only is this recipe delicious, but super healthy and almost a meal in itself. Team it with Kachumber (page 145), Roasted carrot, date and almond salad (page 150) and some Mint chutney (page 164) and you are halfway to attaining nirvana!

PREPARATION TIME
20 minutes (plus soaking/resting time)

COOKING TIME
30 minutes

SERVES
4

हरी मूंग दाल की रोटी

GREEN MUNG ROTI

100 g (3½ oz/½ cup) mung beans

400 g (14 oz/2 cups) atta flour, plus extra for dusting

1 teaspoon salt

4 tablespoons vegan ghee

180–250 ml (6–8½ fl oz/¾–1 cup) warm water

Soak the mung beans in cold water for 6 hours. Drain well.

Combine the drained mung beans, flour, salt, 1 tablespoon of the ghee and enough warm water to make a pliable dough. Knead well until you have a smooth, non-sticky dough. Cover and rest for 20 minutes.

Divide the dough into 10–12 small balls. Roll out each ball, gently dusting with extra flour, to obtain a round shape about 1 cm (½ inch) thick.

Heat a heavy-based frying pan and cook the rotis on both sides, smearing each side with a teaspoon of the remaining ghee, until golden. (This should take 2–3 minutes for each roti.) Serve hot.

PREPARATION TIME
20 minutes

COOKING TIME
30 minutes

MAKES
6–8

---

150 g (5½ oz/1 cup) atta flour or plain (all-purpose) flour (see Note)

55 g (2 oz/½ cup) besan (chickpea flour)

½ teaspoon chilli flakes

pinch of asafoetida

½–1 teaspoon salt, or to taste

1 tablespoon dried fenugreek leaves

vegan ghee or vegan plain yoghurt to serve

In North India, many kinds of flour are used to make breads. This is a part of India where hardly any rice is eaten at all. Atta (from durum wheat), corn, besan (chickpea flour), millet, rye, ragi (from finger millet) and other flours all produce hearty, peasant-style breads. Missie roti is a rustic, home-style spicy flat bread, low in carbohydrates, that highlights the nutty flavour of besan. Serve with vegan plain yoghurt for a quick snack, breakfast or brunch.

मस्सिी रोटी
MISSIE ROTI

Put the flour, besan, chilli, asafoetida and salt in a large bowl. Crush the fenugreek leaves between your hands and add to the bowl, then mix together. Gradually pour in 190 ml (6½ fl oz/¾ cup) water while working the ingredients together, adding a little more water if necessary to make a flexible dough that does not stick to the sides of the bowl. Turn out onto a lightly floured work surface and knead for 10 minutes, or until pliable but not sticky. Place the dough in a clean bowl, cover with a damp cloth and rest for 30 minutes.

Divide the dough into 6–8 balls, each about the size of a golf ball. On a lightly floured work surface, roll out each piece of dough until it is thin like a tortilla and about 6–8 cm (2½ in–3¼ in) in diameter. (This dough is not elastic, and so the roti may be irregular or slightly cracked, which suits this rustic, strongly flavoured bread.)

Heat a heavy-based frying pan over a medium heat. Dry-cook each roti for about 1 minute, then turn and cook the other side for a further 1 minute. The bread is done when it lightens in colour and little brown flecks appear on the surface.

Spread each roti with a little ghee before serving, or serve with yoghurt on the side.

NOTE: You can use plain flour instead of atta flour, but the rotis will have a slightly different taste and texture.

Onion salad प्याज़ का सलाद	142
Kachumber कचुम्बर	145
Watermelon, radish and crunchy rice salad तरबुज़, मूली और पोहा	147
Mango and pineapple salad आम और अनानास का सलाद	149
Roasted carrot, date and almond salad भुनी हुई गाजर, खजूर और बादाम का सलाद	150
Boondi raita बूंदी रायता	151
Cucumber raita खीरे का रायता	153

Indian food is often perceived as curry and rice alone. In fact, nothing could be further from the truth. An Indian meal relies on many different dishes to add freshness and contrast in taste, texture and temperature. When planning your menu, make sure to include a salad. Whether its a basic combination of sliced vegetables with a squeeze of lemon, a raita or a fruit-based dish, a salad will enhance the other dishes on the table.

Lettuce is not a traditional Indian salad ingredient, but other greens, such as baby spinach, amaranth and fenugreek leaves, are used to add a little bitterness to offset a rich curry. Sprouts are another popular ingredient, and not just lentil or alfalfa; radish and mustard sprouts are commonly used to provide crunch and flavour. In the south of India, cabbage and beetroot feature in cooked or tempered salads.

Raita, a yoghurt and vegetable combination, also falls into the salad category. Raita can include raw or cooked ingredients mixed with roasted, powdered spice or tempered with whole spices and aromatic leaves. Generally served at room temperature, raita can be of a thinner consistency, to moisten rice, or thicker, with chunky ingredients. There is a common fallacy that raita is always made from cucumber. But other vegetables and fruits – including potato, tomato, carrot, okra, beetroot, banana, watermelon, apple and fig – also make tasty raita; just use your favourite seasonal fruit or vegetable with a touch of spice.

PREPARATION TIME
20 minutes

SERVES
4

Most Indians are partial to the crunch of raw red (Spanish) onion in a salad. It adds taste and texture when eaten with curries, kababs or snacks. Other members of the allium family, including shallots, leeks or spring onions (scallions), can be used for variation in texture and flavour. The raw taste of the onion is mitigated by combining it with the acidity of different vinegars or lemon or lime juice.

2 large red (Spanish) onions, sliced

juice of 1 lime

pinch of chaat masala (page 20)

1 tablespoon finely chopped mint leaves

1 tablespoon finely chopped coriander (cilantro) leaves

1 tablespoon finely chopped red or green chilli

½–1 teaspoon salt, or to taste

प्याज का सलाद
ONION SALAD

Toss together the onion, lime juice, chaat masala, mint, coriander, chilli and salt in a serving bowl.

Leave at room temperature for 20 minutes to allow the flavours to combine a little, then serve.

The most humble and the most popular salad, eaten with almost everything, kachumber is made from readily available ingredients and can be thrown together in five minutes. If you wish, other vegetables, such as beetroot, carrots and radish, may be added.

PREPARATION TIME
30 minutes

SERVES
4

कचुम्बर
KACHUMBER

Toss all ingredients together and serve immediately with main dishes, rice and bread.

2 large tomatoes, chopped
1 large cucumber, chopped
1 red (Spanish) onion, chopped
2 green chillies, finely chopped
4 sprigs of coriander (cilantro), finely chopped
juice of 1 lemon or lime
½ teaspoon salt

PREPARATION TIME
30 minutes

COOKING TIME
5 minutes

SERVES
4

2–2½ tablespoons vegetable or sunflower oil

110g (4 oz/½ cup) raw flattened rice (*poha* – see Note)

300g (1 lb/2 cups) peeled and diced watermelon

130g (4½ oz/1 cup) red radish, chopped

40 g (1½ oz/½ cup) chopped spring onions (scallions), including white and green parts

DRESSING

1 teaspoon nigella (kalonji)

1 tablespoon mustard oil

½ teaspoon sea salt

1 tablespoon rice wine vinegar

Watermelon is a fabulous salad ingredient. Here, its crisp sweetness teams beautifully with the pungency of the radish, while the crunchy rice provides the perfect balance. With a mustard oil, toasted nigella seed and rice vinegar dressing, you can eat this salad all by itself. Sometimes, I add some pink grapefruit segments for a little bitterness, which really gets the appetite going.

तरबूज़, मूली और पोहा

WATERMELON, RADISH AND CRUNCHY RICE SALAD

In a small wok, heat the oil over a medium heat. Add the flattened rice and stir vigorously as the rice cooks (this will only take a few minutes). Remove from the wok and set aside.

For the dressing, lightly toast the nigella in a frying pan over a medium heat. Add to the mustard oil, salt and vinegar and mix well.

Mix together the watermelon, radish and spring onions, then toss with the dressing. Serve on a bed of the crispy rice.

NOTE: *Poha* is made by dehusking and parboiling white rice, then passing it through rollers to flatten it. Quick cooking, it retains many more nutrients than regular rice and is especially suitable for diabetics. It is available in Indian grocery stores.

PREPARATION TIME
30 minutes

COOKING TIME
5 minutes

SERVES
4

2 dried whole red chillies
¼ teaspoon black mustard seeds
60 ml (2 fl oz/¼ cup) unsweetened pineapple juice
1 mango, peeled and stone removed, diced
1 small pineapple, peeled and central core removed, diced
125 g (4½ oz) fresh coconut flesh, diced
½ teaspoon finely chopped fresh ginger
juice of 1 lime
80 g (2¾ oz/½ cup) unsalted roasted peanuts (optional)

TEMPERING

1 tablespoon vegetable or sunflower oil
1 teaspoon black mustard seeds
10 curry leaves

Salads are eaten with the meal all over India, especially in the north, south and west. They provide a fresh, crisp, sweet, sour or tangy taste, as well as textural excitement, contrasting well with, and helping to cut through, the richness of Indian food. Salads may be cooked or raw, using vegetables, fruits, sprouted lentils or even puffed or flattened rice. Most people outside of India do not appreciate the wide variety of salad dishes eaten routinely in Indian homes. Serve this tangy, sweet, spicy salad as an accompaniment to a meal or as an appetiser.

आम और अनानास का सलाद

MANGO AND PINEAPPLE SALAD

Heat the chillies in a heavy-based frying pan over a medium heat for 1 minute. Remove from the heat and allow to cool, then grind finely with the mustard seeds using a mortar and pestle or an electric spice grinder.

Transfer to a large bowl and gradually whisk in the pineapple juice. (Whisk vigorously so the juice forms an emulsion with the spices, rather than being a liquid with bits of spice floating in it.) Add the mango, pineapple, coconut and ginger, pour over the lime juice and toss to combine well.

To make the tempering, heat the oil in a small frying pan over a medium heat. Add the mustard seeds and curry leaves and heat until they begin to crackle.

Scatter the peanuts, if using, over the salad, then immediately pour the tempering over and serve.

Another one of those almost-a-meal salads, this roasted carrot salad ticks all the boxes: sweet, nutty, roasty, toasty, creamy and delicious. Choose the freshest carrots – if you can get the heirloom variety, even better. Eat this salad with Lemon rice (page 117) or Mushroom and chickpea pulao (page 121) for a marriage made in heaven.

PREPARATION TIME
15 minutes

COOKING TIME
40 minutes

SERVES
4

भुनी हुई गाजर, खजूर और बादाम का सलाद

ROASTED CARROT, DATE AND ALMOND SALAD

200 g (10½ oz/2 cups) thickly sliced carrots (or whole heirloom carrots if you can get them)

2 tablespoons vegetable or sunflower oil

60 g (2 oz/½ cup) slivered almonds

30 g (1oz/¼ cup) dried melon seeds (see Notes)

40 g (1½ oz/¼ cup) pitted dates, sliced (see Notes)

60 g (2 oz/¼ cup) vegan yoghurt

90 g (3 oz/¼ cup) palm syrup

Preheat the oven to 180°C (360°F).

Place the carrots in a roasting tray, drizzle with the oil and roast in the oven until caramelised and tender.

Roast the almonds on a tray in the oven, but only for a few minutes, until lightly browned.

Roast the melon seeds on a tray in the oven for 2 minutes, or until pale golden.

Combine the roasted carrots, almonds and melon seeds with the dates.

Dollop spoonfuls of the yoghurt on the salad but do not mix. Dribble with palm syrup and serve warm.

NOTES: Dried melon seeds, which are available in most Indian grocery stores, can be sprinkled on naan before cooking, or on salads or steamed vegetables for added texture and flavour. They have a high protein content and are rich in many vitamins.

Use fresh dates for this recipe if you can get them, but if you can't, good-quality dried dates will also work well..

PREPARATION TIME
20 minutes

COOKING TIME
30 minutes

SERVES
4 (makes 500 ml/17 fl oz/2 cups)

BOONDIS

110 g (4 oz/1 cup) besan (chickpea flour)

pinch of salt

vegetable or sunflower oil for deep-frying

RAITA

250 g (9 oz/1 cup) vegan plain yoghurt

½–1 teaspoon salt, or to taste

½ teaspoon yellow mustard seeds, roasted and ground (page 18)

1 teaspoon cumin seeds, roasted and ground (page 18)

¼ teaspoon red chilli powder

Raitas are yoghurt salads eaten with the main meal to provide a fresh balance for the palate. Vegan plain yoghurt may be combined with raw salad vegetables, steamed or roasted vegetables such as corn or eggplant (aubergine) or fruit. Boondi raita comes from North India. It is a mix of boondis (tiny balls, or droplets, of besan or chickpea flour, deep-fried), plain yoghurt and spices. Even though some people think of raitas as being 'cooling' and thus unspiced, a good raita will always have one or two spices to enhance its main ingredients.

BOONDI RAITA

To make the boondis, whisk together the besan, salt and 125 ml (4 fl oz/½ cup) water in a medium bowl to make a stiff batter.

Heat the oil in a wok or deep-fryer to 200°C (400°F; see page 27). Using a frying spoon with round holes (see Note), get a spoonful of batter, hold it over the wok or deep-fryer (about 10 cm/4 in from the hot oil to avoid splashing) and press down on the batter with a ladle or other object with a flat unbroken surface to force the batter through the holes in the frying spoon. Little balls of batter will drop into the hot oil and solidify immediately. Deep-fry until golden brown, turning frequently with a clean slotted spoon, for about 1 minute. Remove from the oil and drain on kitchen towels. Leave to cool while deep-frying the remaining boondi batter.

Soak the boondis in a bowl of warm water for 10 minutes, until they swell to about double their size. Gently squeeze the boondis to remove excess water, being careful not to break them.

To make the raita, put the yoghurt, boondis, salt and all but a pinch each of the yellow mustard, cumin and chilli in a small bowl. Mix together, then chill in the refrigerator for at least 15 minutes, or until ready to serve.

Transfer the raita to a serving bowl, sprinkle over the remaining pinch of yellow mustard, cumin and chilli and serve.

NOTE: There are boondi spoons specially designed to make this dish, but any frying spoon with round holes will work. Look for a slotted spoon with round holes in Indian and Asian grocery stores.

PREPARATION TIME
20 minutes

SERVES
4 (makes 500 ml/17 fl oz/2 cups)

250 g (9 oz/1 cup) vegan plain yoghurt

½ cucumber, peeled if desired and seeds removed, grated (see Note)

1 tablespoon finely chopped onion

½–1 teaspoon salt, or to taste

1 teaspoon yellow mustard seeds, roasted and ground (page 18)

2 teaspoons cumin seeds, roasted and ground (page 18)

¼ teaspoon red chilli powder

Not many meals in India would be complete without yoghurt in some form. This might be plain yoghurt, a raita or a sweetened yoghurt. Most Indian families set their own yoghurt at home, but a good-quality store-bought vegan yoghurt is a perfectly acceptable alternative. The most popular of all raitas, cucumber raita, goes especially well with vegan curries. Make sure you remove the seeds from the cucumber or use a seedless variety. And any leftover raita will keep in the refrigerator for up to three days.

खीरे का रायता

CUCUMBER RAITA

Put the yoghurt, cucumber, onion, salt and all but a pinch each of the yellow mustard, cumin and chilli in a small bowl. Mix together, then chill in the refrigerator for at least 20 minutes, or until ready to serve.

Transfer the raita to a serving bowl, sprinkle over the remaining pinch of yellow mustard, cumin and chilli and serve.

NOTE: Raitas are meant to be of a pouring consistency – not too thick. But if you prefer a more solid texture and consistency, squeeze the grated cucumber between your palms to remove all the liquid from it before mixing with the yoghurt.

VARIATION: To make a spinach raita, heat 2 teaspoons of sunflower oil in a small frying pan and gently fry 50 g (1¾ oz) baby spinach with ½ teaspoon garlic paste (page 25) and 1 whole red chilli until the spinach has wilted. Leave to cool, then transfer to a small bowl and add the yoghurt, stirring gently to combine. Season to taste and chill for 20 minutes or until ready to serve.

Coconut chutney नारियल की चटनी	158
Dahi chutney दही चटनी	158
Tamarind and ginger chutney इमली और अदरक की चटनी	160
Green chutney हरी चटनी	161
Sesame chutney तिल की चटनी	161
Plum chutney बेर की चटनी	162
Mint chutney पुदीने की चटनी	164
Eggplant chutney बैंगन की चटनी	165
Tomato chutney टमाटर की चटनी	166
Lime juice chutney नींबू के रस की चटनी	168

The diversity of flavours, textures and temperatures in Indian cuisine can, in part, be attributed to the vast array of accompaniments on offer, including chutneys. The term 'chutney' is used very loosely in India and refers not just to store-bought preserved chutneys, but also to homemade fresh fruit and vegetable chutneys; dipping sauces made with fresh herbs; and yoghurts with spice and herb infusions. No Indian meal is complete without some sort of chutney.

The chutneys in this chapter are quick and easy to prepare. In addition to these recipes, try making your own chutneys by experimenting with leftover fruits and vegetables, and surplus garden produce. Once you master the technique, you will never return to store-bought chutneys.

CHUTNEYS

PREPARATION TIME
30 minutes

COOKING TIME
5 minutes

MAKES
250 ml/8½ fl oz/1 cup

45 g (1½ oz/½ cup) shredded (grated dried) coconut or 60 g (2 oz) freshly grated coconut
1 small green chilli
1 teaspoon chopped fresh ginger
½–1 teaspoon salt, or to taste
1 tablespoon vegetable or sunflower oil
12 curry leaves
2 whole dried red chillies
½ teaspoon black mustard seeds

Fresh coconut chutney, just tempered with herbs and spices, has an important place in South Indian cooking. The fresh flavour of coconut gives a soothing feel to snacks and starters. The chutney will keep in the refrigerator for up to two days.

नारियल की चटनी
COCONUT CHUTNEY

Process the coconut, green chilli, ginger and salt in a food processor, adding up to 250 ml (8½ fl oz/1 cup) warm water a little at a time until the mixture forms a finely ground paste. Transfer to a bowl.

Heat the oil in a small frying pan over a medium heat. Add the curry leaves, dried chillies and mustard seeds and heat until they begin to crackle. Immediately pour over the coconut mixture and stir through to combine.

Serve at room temperature.

PREPARATION TIME
30 minutes

MAKES
500 ml/17 fl oz/2 cups)

250 g (9 oz/1 cup) vegan plain yoghurt
1 onion, chopped
2 green chillies, chopped
small handful mint leaves, chopped
small handful coriander (cilantro) leaves, chopped
½–1 teaspoon salt, or to taste

Dahi chutney is a chopped coriander and mint chutney with green chillies and yoghurt. It is quite spicy and is traditionally served with Hyderabadi biryani. It is thicker and chunkier than Green chutney (page 161) – more like a raita in texture. It will keep in the refrigerator for up to two days.

दही चटनी
DAHI CHUTNEY

Mix together the yoghurt, onion, chilli, mint, coriander and salt in a small bowl. Chill the chutney in the refrigerator for 15 minutes to give the flavours time to infuse before serving.

This piquant, sweet-and-sour fresh chutney comes from North India. It is an important part of chaat, the famous street food that brings together crisp, savoury discs made of semolina or plain (all-purpose) flour with roasted vegetables, puffed rice and fried besan (chickpea flour) vermicelli. As well as being an integral part of chaat, this chutney goes well with salads, potato patties, boiled chickpeas, Pakoras (page 38) and Vegetable samosas (page 41). It will keep in the refrigerator for up to two weeks.

इमली और अदरक की चटनी

TARAMIND AND GINGER CHUTNEY

PREPARATION TIME
10 minutes

COOKING TIME
40 minutes

MAKES
250 ml/8½ fl oz/1 cup

100 g (3½ oz) dried tamarind

1 tablespoon chopped fresh ginger

1 teaspoon chilli powder

1 teaspoon chaat masala (page 20)

100 g (3½ oz) sugar

banana slices to garnish

Put the dried tamarind, ginger, chilli powder, chaat masala, sugar and 500 ml (17 fl oz/2 cups) water in a small saucepan. Stir until the sugar has dissolved, then bring to a boil over a high heat. Reduce the heat to low and simmer for 30 minutes.

Strain the mixture through a mesh strainer to give a homogeneous thick liquid, without any seeds, flesh or fibres from the tamarind or ginger. Chill the chutney in the refrigerator for at least 20 minutes, or until ready to serve. Garnish with banana slices before serving.

PREPARATION TIME
40 minutes

MAKES
375 ml/12½ fl oz/1½ cups

25 g (1 oz) chopped mint leaves
25 g (1 oz) chopped coriander (cilantro) leaves
2 green chillies, chopped
1 garlic clove, chopped
1 small onion, chopped
1 tablespoon sugar
1 teaspoon salt
125 g (4½ oz/½ cup) vegan plain yoghurt

Found in almost every Indian restaurant and takeaway, green chutney is the perfect accompaniment for fried foods such as Pakoras (page 38) or Vegetable samosas (page 41), or tandoori foods. Follow this recipe and you will find yourself taken to a whole new flavour level altogether. Serve it chilled with snacks and starters. It will keep in the refrigerator for up to four days.

हरी चटनी

GREEN CHUTNEY

Put the mint, coriander, chilli, garlic, onion, sugar, salt and yoghurt in a food processor and blend together to form a completely smooth paste, with no flecks of chopped herbs visible.

Chill the chutney in the refrigerator for 30 minutes to give the flavours time to infuse before serving.

NOTE: It is important to chop up all the ingredients before blending them so that you can produce the smoothest paste possible using the least amount of liquid. This process will not work efficiently if large bunches of herbs are put in the food processor.

PREPARATION TIME
30 minutes

COOKING TIME
5 minutes

MAKES
190 ml/6½ fl oz/¾ cup

1 tablespoon sesame seeds, roasted and coarsely ground
3 green chillies
large handful mint leaves
1 small onion, chopped
1 tablespoon chopped garlic
2 tablespoons tamarind pulp (page 25)
½–1 teaspoon salt, or to taste

Although not as popular as the ubiquitous Green chutney (page 161), this is nevertheless a deliciously herby, nutty complement to vegetable kababs. It can also be used as a delicious dip for vegetables – an Indian tahini with spice. It will keep in the refrigerator for up to two days.

तलि की चटनी

SESAME CHUTNEY

Put the sesame seeds, chillies, mint, onion, garlic and tamarind in a food processor and process to make a smooth paste. Transfer to a bowl, add the salt and mix well.

Serve at room temperature or chill in the refrigerator until ready to serve.

I love this plum chutney with hot dishes such as Jackfruit kolhapuri (page 91), pungent ones such as Baked mustard broccoli (page 94), or dishes that benefit from a touch of sweetness, such as Vegetable khichadi (page 104). Plum chutney and other fruit chutneys will generally keep in the refrigerator for up to three weeks. They are eaten in larger quantities than their sharper, hotter cousins, and add more liquid to the meal.

PREPARATION TIME
30 minutes

COOKING TIME
60 minutes

MAKES
1 litre/34 fl oz/4 cups

बेर की चटनी
PLUM CHUTNEY

2 tablespoons vegetable or sunflower oil

2.5 cm (1 in) cinnamon stick

4 cloves

1 small onion, diced

500 g (1 lb 2 oz) plums, halved and stoned

220 g (8 oz/1 cup) sugar

1 teaspoon chilli powder

1 tablespoon ginger paste (page 25)

1 tablespoon garlic paste (page 25)

1½ tablespoons white vinegar

Heat the oil in a large saucepan over a medium heat. Sauté the cinnamon, cloves and onion, stirring occasionally, for about 2 minutes, or until the onion is translucent.

Add the plums, sugar, chilli powder, ginger and garlic pastes and vinegar and stir until the sugar has dissolved. Cook for about 45 minutes, or until the plums are soft and almost all of the liquid has evaporated. Remove from the heat.

Leave the chutney to cool before serving. There is no need to remove the whole spices.

Dark green mint chutney is a refreshing, bold dipping sauce that accompanies fried starters such as Pakoras (page 38), Vegetable samosas (page 41) and vegetable kababs. Indian cooking depends on extras such as this, to provide a clean, contrasting flavour. Mint chutney will keep in the refrigerator for up to four days.

PREPARATION TIME
30 minutes

MAKES
250 ml/8½ fl oz/1 cup

पुदीने की चटनी
MINT CHUTNEY

50 g (1¾ oz) mint leaves
juice of 1 lemon or lime
1 clove garlic
1 tablespoon sugar
1 teaspoon salt
2 green chillies

Process the mint, lemon or lime juice, garlic, sugar, salt and chillies with 125 ml (4 fl oz/½ cup) water in a food processor to form a smooth paste.

Chill the chutney in the refrigerator for 20 minutes to give the flavours time to infuse before serving.

PREPARATION TIME
30 minutes

COOKING TIME
25 minutes

MAKES
1 litre/34 fl oz/4 cups

2 eggplants (aubergines)
45 g (1½ oz/½ cup) shredded (grated dried) coconut or 60 g (2 oz) freshly grated coconut
2 whole dried red chillies, roasted
¼ teaspoon ginger paste (page 25)
¼ teaspoon garlic paste (page 25)
2 teaspoons tamarind pulp (page 25)
40 g (1½ oz/¼ cup) unsalted roasted peanuts
2 tablespoons palm syrup or dark brown sugar or molasses
½–1 teaspoon salt, or to taste

Indian homes abound with chutneys, relishes and pickles that add another dimension to everyday eating. Fresh chutneys can be made with any vegetables in season – try carrots, tomatoes, turnips, cauliflower or pumpkin (winter squash) – and are a good way of using up excess garden produce. Vegetable chutneys will generally keep in the refrigerator for about two months. This eggplant chutney, however, must be served fresh, and will only keep in the refrigerator for one day. Serve it as a dip or to accompany an Indian meal.

बैगन की चटनी

EGGPLANT CHUTNEY

Place the eggplant whole in a heavy-based frying pan or chargrill pan over a medium heat, or under the grill (broiler), for about 20 minutes, or until soft and the skin is charred. Turn only once or twice during cooking. Allow to cool, then cut in half. Scoop out the flesh with a spoon, chop roughly and reserve. Discard the skin.

Put the eggplant flesh, coconut, chillies, ginger and garlic pastes, tamarind, peanuts, palm syrup or dark brown sugar or molasses and salt in a food processor and process to form a thick, chunky consistency or, more traditionally, a smooth paste. Serve at room temperature.

PREPARATION TIME
20 minutes

COOKING TIME
20 minutes

MAKES
500 ml/17 fl oz/2 cups

1 tablespoon mustard oil or vegetable or sunflower oil
1 teaspoon panch phoron (page 21)
2 whole dried red chillies
1 tablespoon ginger paste (page 25)
4 large tomatoes, roughly chopped
110 g (4 oz/½ cup) sugar
½–1 teaspoon salt, or to taste

A traditional menu in Bengal always starts with something bitter, using vegetables, and ends with something sweet. This is true whether you are eating an everyday lunch or dinner, or celebrating an event such as a wedding. This sweet but deliciously fresh chutney is a must at the end of a Bengali meal, but you can also serve it alongside a spicy curry to balance out the heat. It will keep in the refrigerator for up to one week.

टमाटर की चटनी

TOMATO CHUTNEY

Heat the oil in a large saucepan over a medium heat. If you are using mustard oil, wait until it is smoking. Heat the panch phoron and chillies until they begin to crackle. Immediately stir in the ginger paste and sauté for 2 minutes.

Stir in the tomato, sugar and salt and cook, stirring occasionally, for 10 minutes, or until the tomato is soft. Remove from the heat and leave to cool.

Serve at room temperature.

PREPARATION TIME
15 minutes

COOKING TIME
40 minutes

MAKES
250 ml/8½ fl oz/1 cup

1 tablespoon vegetable or sunflower oil
½ teaspoon black mustard seeds
250 ml (8½ fl oz/1 cup) lime juice
220 g (8 oz/1 cup) sugar
1 teaspoon asafoetida
1 teaspoon chilli powder
½ teaspoon turmeric
½–1 teaspoon salt, or to taste

Pickles and chutneys add contrasting tastes, textures and temperatures to Indian meals. Most chutney recipes start with whole ingredients, but this one starts with a juice. The resulting syrupy consistency is fantastic for serving as a dipping sauce for Masala pappadums (page 36), or drizzled over Pakoras (page 38), Upma (page 56) or Onion bhajees (page 59). It will keep in the refrigerator for a month.

नीबू के रस की चटनी

LIME JUICE CHUTNEY

Heat the oil in a large saucepan over a medium heat. Add the mustard seeds and heat until they begin to crackle. Immediately add the lime juice, sugar, asafoetida, chilli powder, turmeric and salt and stir until the sugar has dissolved.

Reduce the heat to low and cook, uncovered, for about 30 minutes, or until the liquid has thickened to a syrup.

Cool, then chill in the refrigerator for at least 20 minutes, or until ready to serve.

Passionfruit kulfi पैशनफ्रूट कुल्फी	174
Vermicelli pudding सेवई की खीर	177
Baked saffron yoghurt pudding with tomato compote टमाटर एर भापा दोई	178
Betel leaf chaat with apple and pear pakoras पानवाली फल की चाट, सेव और नाशपति के पकोडे	180
Mango rice pudding with palm syrup अक्की परमन्ना	181
Gujiyas गुझिया	182
Mung dal slice मूंगदाल की बर्फी	183
Orange halwa with sultanas किशमिश और संतरे का हलवा	184
Coconut pancakes पतिशिप्ता	186
Carrot halwa गाजर का हलवा	187

Desserts are not often considered when preparing an everyday Indian meal, as the preceding dishes tend to be rich, with multiple components. A popular way to finish a meal is with a simple bowl of yoghurt, maybe sweetened with jaggery or served with fresh fruit.

However, many Indians do have a sweet tooth and desserts always feature on the menu at special and festive occasions. Kulfi is a perennial favourite that can be easily re-created at home using any variety of fresh fruit – experiment with whatever is in season.

For this chapter I have chosen recipes not only that I love, but that reveal the diversity of Indian desserts – from the simple Coconut pancakes (page 186), to the beautifully rich Vermicelli pudding (page 177), to the cheffy Betel leaf fruit chaat with apple and pear pakoras (page 180), and my own personal creation, Baked saffron yoghurt pudding with tomato compote (page 178). There is no end to the variations you can create from these dessert bases.

DESSERTS

PREPARATION TIME
30 minutes (plus freezing time)

SERVES
6

300 ml (10 fl oz/1¼ cups) vegan thickened cream
300 ml (10 fl oz/1¼ cups) coconut milk
300 ml (10 fl oz/1¼ cups) almond cream
300 ml (10 fl oz/1¼ cups) passionfruit pulp (see Note)
60 g (2 oz/½ cup) almond meal

Kulfi is an Indian almond ice cream, traditionally frozen in conical containers to resemble the Himalayan mountains. In India it is served with falooda, a cornflour (cornstarch) vermicelli, which provides a contrast in temperature, taste and texture. Kulfi is eaten on all sorts of occasions – on a casual beach outing, at the movies, or as a sweet finale to a wedding. This is a hard ice cream and should be transferred from the freezer to the refrigerator five minutes before serving to help remove the kulfi from the mould without it melting.

पैशनफ्रूट कुल्फी

PASSIONFRUIT KULFI

Put the cream, coconut milk, almond cream and 200 ml (7 fl oz/¾ cup) of the passionfruit pulp in a large bowl and stir. Add the almond meal and mix until well combined. Pour the mixture into a freezer-proof 1.5 litre (51 fl oz/6 cup) mould or terrine or into six 250 ml (8½ fl oz/1 cup) ramekins or dessert glasses. Cover with plastic wrap and freeze for at least 8 hours.

About 5 minutes before serving, transfer the kulfi to the refrigerator. When ready to serve, turn the kulfi out of the large mould or terrine onto a platter and cut into slices, or invert the individual ramekins onto plates. (If you are having difficulty getting the kulfi out, roll each ramekin between your hands to provide a little warmth. However, do not run hot water over the ramekins as this will make the surface of the ice cream melt.) If you have prepared the kulfi in dessert glasses, you can serve them as they are.

Spoon the remaining passionfruit pulp over the top of the kulfi and serve immediately.

NOTE: You will need 4–6 fresh passionfruit or you could use tinned passionfruit pulp.

As children, my cousins and I often spent summer holidays with my grandparents at their home in Dehradun, a sprawling country town in the Himalayan foothills. The house was surrounded by lychee, mango, plum and peach orchards, with trees to climb and uninterrupted lazy days of book reading – but best of all, fabulous food prepared by their hugely talented cook, Moti Singh. This dish was a particular highlight – a decadent breakfast cereal or a delicious, comforting dessert.

सेवई की खीर

VERMICELLI PUDDING

PREPARATION TIME
10 minutes

COOKING TIME
45 minutes

SERVES
4–6

400 ml (13½ fl oz) vegan milk

125 ml (4 fl oz/½ cup) vegan thickened cream

55 g (2 oz/¼ cup) sugar

3 saffron threads

4 green cardamom pods, coarsely ground

2 tablespoons sultanas (golden raisins)

100 g (3½ oz) roasted vermicelli (see Note)

chopped shelled pistachio nuts to garnish

Heat the milk in a heavy-based saucepan over a low heat. When it is hot, stir in the cream, sugar, saffron, cardamom and sultanas and simmer for about 30 minutes.

Carefully slide in the vermicelli and cook over a low heat, stirring continuously, for about 15 minutes or until the pudding thickens.

Garnish with the pistachio nuts and serve hot.

NOTE: Roasted vermicelli is available from Indian grocery stores.

VARIATION: For a lighter version of this dish, more appropriate for serving at breakfast, heat the milk and stir in the sugar, saffron, cardamom and sultanas, omitting the cream. Do not simmer for 30 minutes. Instead, add the vermicelli immediately, then continue as above.

PREPARATION TIME
15 minutes

COOKING TIME
35 minutes

SERVES
4

---

4 ripe tomatoes, chopped

1 teaspoon ginger paste (page 25)

220 g (8 oz/1 cup) sugar

250 g (9 oz/1 cup) vegan plain yoghurt

200 g (7 oz/⅔ cup) vegan condensed milk

60 ml (2 fl oz/¼ cup) vegan thickened cream

1 teaspoon saffron infusion (page 21)

Sweetened yoghurt, in its many guises, is a popular dessert in Bengal, where the sweet shops are full of little terracotta pots brimming with caramelised yoghurt. This dish was first made at the Spice Kitchen many years ago, and this particular interpretation of a sweetened yoghurt is all mine. The unusual partnership of tomato and yoghurt works really well.

टमाटर एर भापा दोई

BAKED SAFFRON YOGHURT PUDDING WITH TOMATO COMPOTE

Preheat the oven to 160°C (320°F).

Mix together the tomato, ginger paste and sugar in a medium saucepan over a medium heat and cook for about 8–10 minutes, or until the tomato has softened. Spread out over the base of a 25 x 12 cm (10 x 4¾ in) ovenproof dish.

Mix together the yoghurt, condensed milk, cream and saffron infusion in a medium bowl.

Pour the yoghurt mixture over the tomato mixture and bake in the oven for 20–35 minutes, or until the pudding is just set. When the pudding is cooked, it will look smooth like a panna cotta, but it will still be a little wobbly. It is important not to cook it for any longer once it reaches this stage, because overcooking will make it curdle and the water separate.

Chill in the refrigerator for 1 hour (the pudding will become firmer and lose its wobbliness) before serving.

NOTE: For individual serves, assemble the pudding in ovenproof glasses and bake for 20 minutes before chilling.

PREPARATION TIME
45 minutes

COOKING TIME
30 minutes

SERVES
4–6

---

sunflower oil for deep-frying

4 fresh betel leaves (see Notes)

½ teaspoon chaat masala (page 20) to garnish

icing (confectioners') sugar to garnish

FRUIT CHAAT

50 g (¼ cup/1¾ oz) banana, peeled and diced

50 g (¼ cup/1¾ oz) honeydew melon, diced (see Note)

50 g (¼ cup/1¾ oz) rockmelon (canteloupe), diced

50 g (¼ cup/1¾ oz) pineapple, diced

50 g (¼ cup/1¾ oz) cucumber, diced

1 tablespoon Mint chutney (page 164)

1 tablespoon Tamarind and ginger chutney (page 160)

PAKORAS

55 g (2 oz/½ cup) besan (chickpea flour)

90 g (3 oz/½ cup) rice flour (fine)

pinch of salt

1 apple (granny smith or other tart variety), thinly sliced

1 pear (D'Anjou, nashi or other hard variety), thinly sliced

This is a dessert for those who don't like dessert. The slightly hot taste of the crisp betel leaf is soothed by the sweetness of the fruit and the contrasting tang of the mint and tamarind. Accompanied by the crunchy, just-fried sweet/savoury pakoras, this dish makes a refreshing end to a rich meal, or a delicious brunch or afternoon tea treat.

पानवाली फल की चाट, सेव और नाशपत्ती के पकोड़े

BETEL LEAF FRUIT CHAAT WITH APPLE AND PEAR PAKORAS

To make the fruit chaat, combine the fruit and cucumber with the two chutneys. Set aside.

To make the pakoras, heat the oil in a wok or deep-fryer to 180°C (360°F). Whisk the besan and rice flours together with the salt and enough cold water to obtain a coating consistency. Dip the sliced apple and pear into the batter one piece at a time and fry in small batches until crisp. Drain the pakoras on paper towels and, while still hot, dredge with icing sugar..

To serve, place a spoonful of fruit chaat on each betel leaf and sprinkle with chaat masala. Arrange the leaves on a serving platter and.serve alongside the hot pakoras..

NOTES: The fruit for the chaat can be varied according to the season. Tropical fruit like guava and lychees are especially delicious.

Betel leaves are available in most Indian grocery stores.

PREPARATION TIME
20 minutes

COOKING TIME
25 minutes

SERVES
4

---

2 ripe mangoes, plus extra to garnish

200 g (7½ oz/1 cup) well-cooked short-grain rice

350 g (7½ oz/1 cup) palm syrup

5–6 tablespoons raw cashew nuts

5–6 tablespoons sultanas (golden raisins)

250 ml (8½ fl oz/1 cup) coconut milk

1 teaspoon cardamom pods, crushed

½ teaspoon freshly grated nutmeg

A popular home-style dessert, rice pudding can be found in many forms throughout India, using coconut milk or milk, palm syrup or rice flour. This summer version, with its delectable mango flavour, is a show stopper. For something very different, instead of ripe mango pulp, try using green mango pulp, which must be cooked with sugar beforehand.

अक्की परमन्ना

MANGO RICE PUDDING WITH PALM SYRUP

Peel the mangoes and, using a sharp knife, remove all the flesh from around the stone. Reserving some pieces for garnish, process the rest of the flesh in a food processor until it forms a smooth pulp. Set aside.

In a heavy-based saucepan, mix together the cooked rice, palm syrup, cashew nuts, sultanas and coconut milk. Cook over a low heat, stirring constantly.

When the rice is soft and creamy (this should only take about 15 minutes), stir in the cardamom and nutmeg. Remove from the heat and leave to cool to room temperature, then chill in the refrigerator for 20 minutes.

When chilled, stir the mango pulp through the rice pudding. Divide between four dessert glasses, garnish with the reserved mango pieces and serve.

VARIATION: If you want to make a very different-flavoured version with green mango, you will need 250 g (9 oz) green mango (you can buy this from Indian grocery stores during spring and early summer). Steam the whole mango in a steamer basket over a saucepan of simmering water for 30 minutes, or until soft. Allow to cool, then, using a very sharp knife, peel the skin, and slice away all the flesh from the stone. Put the flesh and 100 g (3½ oz) sugar in a food processor and blend to make a pulp. Stir the pulp through the chilled rice pudding and serve.

India is a land of festivals. Diwali, Holi, Onam, Durga Puja ... all celebrate the victory of good over evil. Giant marquees take over parks, streets are cordoned off, vendors set up a kaleidoscope of stalls. People wander along in their flash new clothes, munching into delicious, sugar-loaded sweets. If you can't be there, you can still enjoy these sweet, nut-filled pastries, as gujiyas are easy enough to make at home with the kids, who will devour them. They can be made in bulk and stored in the refrigerator for a few days.

गुझिया

GUJIYAS

PREPARATION TIME
40 minutes

COOKING TIME
30 minutes

SERVES
4

- 4 sheets ready-made vegan shortcrust (pie) pastry
- 100 g (3½ oz/1 cup) vegan milk powder
- 65 g (2¼ oz/¾ cup) shredded (grated dried) coconut
- 30 g (1 oz/¼ cup) slivered almonds
- 30 g (1 oz/¼ cup) semolina
- 30 g (1 oz/¼ cup) sultanas (golden raisins)
- ½ teaspoon freshly ground green cardamom
- 125 g (4½ oz/½ cup) vegan cream cheese
- sunflower oil for deep-frying

DIPPING SYRUP
- 250 g (9oz/1¼ cups) sugar

To make the dipping syrup, put the sugar and 400 ml (13½ fl oz) of water in a medium saucepan and cook over a high heat until the sugar has dissolved. Remove from the heat immediately and cool.

Cut four small rounds about 8 cm (3¼ in) in diameter out of each pastry sheet, so that you have sixteen rounds altogether. Mix together the milk powder, coconut, almonds, semolina, sultanas and cardamom, adding enough cream cheese to hold the mixture together. Place a little of the filling in each pastry round and seal into a semicircle. You can press the edges together with a fork or crimp the edges like a Cornish pastie.

Heat the oil in a wok or deep-fryer to 180°C (360°F). Deep-fry the gujiyas a few at a time, until golden brown. Remove and drain on paper towels. Dip in syrup and serve immediately or store at room temperature for later.

PREPARATION TIME
25 minutes

COOKING TIME
60 minutes

SERVES
4–6

---

250 g (9 oz/1¼ cups) mung dal (split dried mung beans), soaked for 2 hours

250 g (9 oz/1 cup) vegan ghee

250 g (9 oz/1¼ cups) sugar

1 teaspoon freshly ground cardamom

200 g (7 oz/2 cups) walnuts to garnish

This is a delicious, gluten-free lentil slice inspired by the cooking of Rajasthan. A recipe for celebrations and festive eating, it may be served hot or cold, but is especially nice hot, and guaranteed to chase away the winter chills. It can be made ahead of time and stores well in the refrigerator. Serve with vegan cream or ice cream.

मूंगदाल की बर्फी
MUNG DAL SLICE

Drain the dal and process in a food processor until coarsely ground. Heat the ghee in an heavy-based saucepan over a low heat. Add the dal and stir until it turns golden brown.

In a separate heavy-based saucepan, bring 750 ml (25½ fl oz/3 cups) water to a boil, then add the sugar. When the sugar is completely dissolved, add the dal. Cook over a low heat, stirring regularly, until the mixture is thick and porridge-like. Add the cardamom and mix well. Pour into a shallow baking tray. Press down and sprinkle the walnuts on top.

When cool, cut into squares or diamonds. Serve as is or, to serve hot, reheat in a warm oven (140° Celsius) for 8 minutes, or microwave each piece for 30 seconds on high.

Halwas have Turkish and Middle Eastern ancestry, and many different versions can be found throughout India, some of them truly, uniquely Indian. This halwa – a lovely, warm, citrusy pudding made with semolina in just minutes – is the ultimate winter dessert. It is also perfect for afternoon tea.

PREPARATION TIME
30 minutes

COOKING TIME
15 minutes

SERVES
4

किशमिश और संतरे का हलवा
ORANGE HALWA WITH SULTANAS

60 g (2 oz) vegan ghee

125 g (4½ oz/1 cup) semolina

110 g (4 oz/½ cup) sugar

2 tablespoons sultanas (golden raisins)

190 ml (6½ fl oz/¾ cup) freshly squeezed orange juice, from 2–3 oranges

1 tablespoon grated orange zest

125 ml (4 fl oz/½ cup) vegan milk (or substitute with water)

orange segments to garnish

Heat the ghee in a large frying pan over a medium heat. Cook the semolina, stirring continuously, for about 5 minutes, or until it starts to brown.

Add the sugar and sultanas and cook, stirring, for 1 minute. Add the orange juice and zest and mix together thoroughly, then cook for 2 minutes.

Pour in the milk (or water) and cook, stirring vigorously, for 8–10 minutes, or until the liquid is completely absorbed.

Garnish with the orange segments and serve hot.

Indian sweets are served not only at the end of the meal, they are eaten as a snack at any time of day! A favourite in Bengal, this is a simple recipe of thin, crepe-like pancakes filled with a juicy coconut filling – a lovely summer mouthful. They are really very easy to cook, and you might find that the pancakes disappear as soon as you make them.

पतश्रिप्ता
COCONUT PANCAKES

PREPARATION TIME
20 minutes

COOKING TIME
30 minutes

SERVES
4

BATTER

150 g (5½ oz/1 cup) plain (all-purpose) flour

250–300 ml (8½–10 fl oz) vegan milk

15 g (½ oz) vegan ghee or 1 tablespoon vegetable or sunflower oil

COCONUT FILLING

2 tablespoons vegan powdered milk

45 g (1½ oz/½ cup) shredded (grated dried) coconut

2 tablespoons sugar

100 ml (3½ fl oz) vegan thickened cream

To make the batter, sift the flour into a large bowl and make a well in the centre. Add 200 ml (7 fl oz) of the milk and the ghee or oil and whisk together to make a thin, smooth batter, adding the remaining milk as necessary to form the right consistency. Rest for 20 minutes.

Meanwhile, make the coconut filling. Mix together the powdered milk, coconut, sugar and cream in a small bowl until the powdered milk has dissolved and the filling is thick and chunky. Set aside.

Spray a medium non-stick frying pan with olive or canola oil and heat over a medium heat. Pour in a ladleful of the batter and swirl it around to coat the base of the pan, forming a thin, crepe-like pancake about 10 cm (4 in) in diameter. Cook for 2 minutes. Flip and cook on the other side for 5–10 seconds. Transfer the pancake to a large plate and leave to cool. Repeat with the remaining batter.

When cool, lay each pancake out on a work surface. Place about 2 tablespoons of coconut filling across one end, then roll up the pancake to enclose the filling.

Cut each pancake into 3–4 pieces and serve cold.

PREPARATION TIME
30 minutes

COOKING TIME
75 minutes

SERVES
4

---

310 g (11 oz) grated carrot

500 ml (17 fl oz/2 cups) vegan milk

220 g (8 oz/1 cup) sugar

125 g (4½ oz) vegan ghee or vegan butter

4 green cardamom pods, crushed

100 g (3½ oz/½ cup) vegan powdered milk

shelled pistachio nuts to garnish

Halwas are enjoyed all over India. Beetroot (beets), zucchini (courgettes), pumpkin (winter squash) or lentils can all be used as the main ingredient. They can be found in many forms but are usually cooked to a rough mash. Eaten warm, they are the closest thing to a pudding, Indian-style. This winter warmer is a North Indian favourite, and you could double or even triple the quantities I've given as it will keep for up to two weeks in the refrigerator. Heat it up just before serving.

गाजर का हलवा
CARROT HALWA

Mix together the carrot and milk in a large heavy-based saucepan over a medium heat. Bring almost to a boil, then reduce the heat to low and cook, stirring occasionally, for about 1 hour, or until the carrot has absorbed all the milk.

Stir in the sugar, increase the heat to medium and cook for 10 minutes, or until the mixture is dry. Stir in the ghee or butter, then cook, stirring occasionally, for 7 minutes, or until the mixture takes on a glossy appearance.

Add the cardamom and powdered milk and stir through to combine well.

Garnish with the pistachio nuts and serve warm.

GLOSSARY

ALMOND CREAM
Available commercially, a good substitute for dairy cream in Indian recipes.

ATTA FLOUR
A whole-wheat flour that includes every component of the grain (the bran, the germ and the endosperm). Its high gluten content provides elasticity, meaning that dough made from atta flour is strong and can be rolled into thin sheets.

BANANA CHILLI
A medium-sized member of the chilli pepper family with a mild, tangy taste. While typically bright yellow, banana chilllies can change to green, red and orange as they ripen. Often pickled, stuffed or eaten raw.

BESAN
A gluten-free flour made from chickpeas; high in protein and carbohydrates.

BHUNA
A method of frying spices in oil and other ingredients with a minimum of water to give curries a complex, roasted flavour. Recipes such as Kum kum tamatar (page 70), Mixed vegetable navratan curry (page 74), Smoky eggplant bhurta (page 82) and Cauliflower masala (page 93) use this method.

COCONUT MILK
See page 26 for notes on fresh coconut milk and how to make it. If necessary, tinned coconut milk can be substituted, but fresh produces a better flavour.

COCONUT OIL
A natural oil derived from the kernels, meat and milk of the coconut palm fruit. Gives a subtle aroma of coconut to recipes. Like olive oil, coconut oil must be stored in a cool, dark place to keep it fresh and to retain its nutritional value and flavour.

CURRY LEAVES
Belong to the citrus family and impart a fresh, unique flavour and aroma.

DRIED FIGS
Available commercially, a good source of calcium and potassium, and rich in fibre.

DRUMSTICKS
Another name for the pods of the moringa tree, which are considered to have many health benefits. Add to soups, stews and curries.

FRIED ONIONS
Also called *birista*, fried onions are used in many Indian recipes as a garnish, as an important component in biryani, or as a spice paste (ground). They are made by frying thinly sliced onions at a low temperature until golden brown and crispy.

JACKFRUIT
Belongs to the fig, mulberry and breadfruit family. Green jackfruit has a mild taste and a meaty texture. When ripe, it is sweet and used in desserts. Tinned jackfruit is widely available.

JAGGERY
A solid, unrefined, reduced cane sugar product used to add sweetness to savoury and sweet recipes or eaten on its own. Jaggery has a unique taste and there is no real substitute. It is widely available at Indian grocery stores, but if you're unable to obtain it, replace with palm syrup.

KADHI
A soupy curry thickened with chickpea flour.

KARAHI
A traditional round-based pan, similar to an Asian wok but slightly deeper and made from a thicker metal, such as cast iron. Available in larger Indian grocery stores.

MASOOR DAL
Split red lentils, quick cooking and easily digested.

MUSTARD OIL
A pungent oil with a sharp mustard taste. Known for its antibacterial, antifungal and anti-inflammatory properties.

PALM SYRUP
A natural sweetener made from the nectar of coconut flower blossoms; use as a vegan substitute for honey.

PAPPADUM
A wafer-thin disc, prepared from a flour or paste derived from lentils, chickpeas, sago, rice, etc., then fried or grilled. Served as a snack or an accompaniment to a main dish.

RIDGE GOURD
Also known as Chinese okra. Its spiky exterior is peeled away to reveal a tender, moist interior.

SEMOLINA
Made from durum wheat. Less refined than plain flour, it has a nutty taste and a coarse texture.

SHORBA
A soup or a thick gravy in Mughal cooking.

SILKEN TOFU
A Japanese-style tofu with a softer consistency than regular tofu; available in soft, medium, firm and extra firm.

TAMARIND
An evergreen tree of the pea family; it has a sweet and sour pulp that is very versatile in both sweet and savoury recipes.

TANDOOR
Introduced to north-west India during the Mughal invasion in the fourteenth century, the tandoor is a clay oven fired with charcoal. A variety of breads can be cooked on its sides, where the heat is more than 400° Celsius. (750° Fahrenheit). Modern tandoors may be set inside a stainless steel frame and insulated with fibreglass.

TEMPERING
Also knows as *tadka* or *baghar*. A process of heating spices or other aromatics in oil or ghee, and adding the mixture to a dish to enrich its flavour, at either the start or the end of the method.

URAD DAL
Black gram (white when its skin is removed), with a unique flavour, different to the other lentils. High in folate and other nutrients, it is an essential ingredient in the dosa (a South Indian pancake).

VEGAN SUBSTITUTES
See page 28 for notes on vegan butter, condensed milk, cream, ghee, milk and milk powders.

GLOSSARY

INDEX

A
ajwain seeds 17
Akbar 11
allspice 17
almond cream 191
almonds
   Gujiyas 182
   Mushroom and chickpea pulao 121
   Passionfruit kulfi 176
   Roasted carrot, date and almond salad 150
amchur 17
apple and pear pakoras 180
asafoetida 17
Ashoka 11
atta flour 191

B
Baked mustard broccoli 94
Baked saffron yoghurt pudding with tomato compote 178
Balti masala 21
   Karahi-style baby spinach and mushrooms 88
banana chilli 191
Banana chilli and potato pakoras 51
beans, green
   Green bean thoran 67
   Mixed vegetable Navratan curry 74
   Sambar dal 100
   Vegetable biryani 64
   Vegetable chakka 77
   Vegetable khichadi 104
   Vegetable medley with panch phoron 76
   Vegetable moilee 92
   Vegetable samosas 41
beans, kidney
   Rajma dal 105
Beetroot and vegetable 'chops' 55
besan (chickpea flour) 191
   Banana chilli and potato pakoras 51
   Betel leaf fruit chaat with apple and pear pakoras 180
   Boondi raita 151
   Cabbage bondas 49
   Dahi ke kababs 50
   Missie roti 137
   Onion bhajees 59
   Pakoras 38
   Spinach kadhi 111
Betel leaf fruit chaat with apple and pear pakoras 180
bhajees, Onion 59
Bhaturas 133
bhuna 191
bhurta
   Smoky eggplant bhurta 82
   Sweet potato and turnip bhurta 75
biryani, Vegetable 64
Black peppercorn and cumin rice 118
bondas, Cabbage 49
Boondi raita 151
breads 115
   Bhaturas 133
   Chapattis 131
   Green mung roti 136
   Missie roti 137
   Naan 128
   Parathas 134
   Pooris 132
breakfasts
   Grilled Swiss brown mushrooms with spiced breadcrumbs and green peas 53
   Missie roti 137
   Onion uthappams 46
   Upma 56
   Vermicelli pudding 177
broccoli, Baked mustard 94
Buddhism 11
butter 28

C
cabbage
   Cabbage bondas 49
   Mixed vegetable Navratan curry 74
   Vegetable medley with panch phoron 76
capsicums
   Cauliflower masala 93
   Vegetable medley with panch phoron 76
cardamom 17
carrots
   Beetroot and vegetable 'chops' 55
   Carrot halwa 187
   Mixed vegetable Navratan curry 74

Mulligatawny soup 42
Roasted carrot, date and almond salad 150
Vegetable biryani 64
Vegetable khichadi 104
Vegetable moilee 92
Vegetable samosas 41
cashew nuts
   Kum kum tamatar 70
   Lemon rice 117
   Mango rice pudding with palm syrup 181
   Mushroom and chickpea pulao 121
   Vegetable biryani 64
cauliflower
   Cauliflower masala 93
   Mixed vegetable Navratan curry 74
   Pakoras 38
   Sambar dal 100
   Vegetable biryani 64
   Vegetable chakka 77
   Vegetable khichadi 104
   Vegetable medley with panch phoron 76
   Vegetable samosas 41
   chaat (fruit), Betel leaf 180
Chaat masala 20
   Betel leaf fruit chaat with apple and pear pakoras 180
   Masala pappadums 36
   Onion salad 142
   Tamarind and ginger chutney 160
chakka, Vegetable 77
Chana dal with coconut and zucchini 109
Chapattis 131
chickpeas 99
   Chickpea masala 103
   Mushroom and chickpea pulao 121
   see also besan, chana dal
chilli (Banana) and potato pakoras 51

'chops', Beetroot and vegetable 55
chutneys 156–7
   Coconut chutney 158
   Dahi chutney 158
   Eggplant chutney 165
   Green chutney 161
   Lime juice chutney 169
   Mint chutney 164
   Plum chutney 162
   Sesame chutney 161
   Tamarind and ginger chutney 160
   Tomato chutney 166
cinnamon 17
cloves 18
coconut, fresh 26
   Chana dal with coconut and zucchini 109
   Coconut chutney 158
   Eggplant chutney 165
   Green bean thoran 67
   Mango and pineapple salad 149
   Masala pappadums 37
coconut milk 191
   Baked mustard broccoli 94
   Fresh coconut milk 26
   Mango rice pudding with palm syrup 181
   Mulligatawny soup 42
   Mushroom and coconut shorba 43
   Passionfruit kulfi 176
   Vegetable moilee 92
coconut oil 191
Coconut pancakes 186
condensed milk 28
coriander 18
corn
   Corn takatak 68
   Vegetable samosas 41
cream 28
Crispy straw potatoes 127
cucumbers
   Betel leaf fruit chaat with apple and pear pakoras 180

Cucumber raita 153
Kachumber 145
cumin 18
curry, Mixed vegetable Navratan 74
curry leaves 191

D
Dahi chutney 158
Dahi ke kababs 50
dals
   Chana dal with coconut and zucchini 109
   Masoor dal tarkewali 107
   Pahari dal 110
   Rajma dal 105
   Sambar dal 100
date and almond salad, Roasted carrot 150
deep-frying 27
desserts 172–3
   Baked saffron yoghurt pudding with tomato compote 178
   Betel leaf fruit chaat with apple and pear pakoras 180
   Carrot halwa 187
   Coconut pancakes 186
   Gujiyas 182
   Mango rice pudding with palm syrup 181
   Mung dal slice 183
   Orange halwa with sultanas 184
   Passionfruit kulfi 176
   Vermicelli pudding 177
dhungar method 28
drumsticks 191
   Vegetable moilee 92

E

eggplant
- Eggplant chutney 165
- Kum kum tamatar 70
- Pakoras 38
- Sambar dal 100
- Smoky eggplant bhurta 82
- Vegetable biryani 64
- Vegetable chakka 77

F

- fennel seeds 18
- fenugreek 18
- figs, dried 191
- figs, Tomatoes filled with mushrooms and 83
- Fresh coconut milk 26
- fruit chaat (Betel leaf) with apple and pear pakoras 180

G

- Gandhi 11
- Garam masala 20
- Garlic paste 25
- ghee 28
- ginger chutney, Tamarind and 160
- Ginger paste 25
- Green bean thoran 67
- Green chutney 161
- Green mung roti 136
- Green peas with ginger and lemon 81
- Grilled Swiss brown mushrooms with spiced breadcrumbs and green peas 53
- Gujiyas 182

H

halwa
- Carrot halwa 187
- Orange halwa with sultanas 184

Hinduism 10–11

I

ice cream *see* kulfi

J

jackfruit 191
- Jackfruit kolhapuri 91

jaggery 191
Jainism 11

K

- kababs, Dahi ke 50
- Kachumber 145
- kadhi 111, 191
- karahi 29, 191
- Karahi-style baby spinach and mushrooms 88
- kewra essence 70
- khichadi, Vegetable 104
- kulfi, Passionfruit 176
- Kum kum tamatar 70

L

Lemon rice 117
lentils 99
   see also chana dal, masoor dal, mung dal, urad dal
Lime juice chutney 169

M

mace 18
mangoes
- Mango and pineapple salad 149
- Mango rice pudding with palm syrup 181

Masala pappadums 37
masoor dal 192
- Masoor dal tarkewali 107
- Masoor dal wadas 57
- Mulligatawny soup 42
- Sambar dal 100
- Vegetable khichadi 104

milk 28
milk powders 28
Mint chutney 164
Missie roti 137
Mixed vegetable Navratan curry 74
moilee, Vegetable 92
Mulligatawny soup 42
mung dal, split
- Mung dal slice 183
- Vegetable khichadi 104

mung dal, whole
- Green mung roti 136

mushrooms
- Grilled Swiss brown mushrooms with spiced breadcrumbs and green peas 53
- Karahi-style baby spinach and mushrooms 88
- Mushroom and chickpea pulao 121
- Mushroom and coconut shorba 43
- Tomatoes filled with mushrooms and figs 83
- Vegetable biryani 64

mustard 18
mustard broccoli, Baked 94
mustard oil 192

N

Naan 128
Navratan curry 74
nutmeg 18
nuts 63

O

Okra do pyaz 86
Onion bhajees 59
Onion salad 142
onion seeds 18
Onion uthappams 46

onions, fried 191
Orange halwa with sultanas 184

P
Pahari dal 110
pakoras
   Banana chilli and potato pakoras 51
   Betel leaf fruit chaat with apple and pear pakoras 180
   Pakoras 38
palm syrup 192
pancakes, Coconut 186
Panch phoron 21
   Pumpkin with panch phoron 73
   Tomato chutney 166
   Vegetable chakka 77
   Vegetable medley with panch phoron 76
Pao bhajee 44
pappadums 36, 192
Farathas 134
Passionfruit kulfi 176
pastries
   Gujiyas 182
   Vegetable samosas 41
peanuts
   Beetroot and vegetable 'chops' 55
   Eggplant chutney 165
   Lemon rice 117
   Mango and pineapple salad 149
pear pakoras, apple and 180
peas
   Beetroot and vegetable 'chops' 55
   Green peas with ginger and lemon 81
   Grilled Swiss brown mushrooms with spiced breadcrumbs and green peas 53
   Mixed vegetable Navratan curry 74

Vegetable biryani 64
Vegetable medley with panch phoron 76
Vegetable samosas 41
pepper 18
pineapple
   Betel leaf fruit chaat with apple and pear pakoras 180
   Mango and pineapple salad 149
Plum chutney 162
Pooris 132
Poppy seed potatoes 126
poppy seeds 19
potatoes 115
   Banana chilli and potato pakoras 51
   Beetroot and vegetable 'chops' 55
   Crispy straw potatoes 127
   Jackfruit kolhapuri 91
   Mixed vegetable Navratan curry 74
   Pakoras 38
   Pao bhajee 44
   Poppy seed potatoes 126
   Potatoes with cumin seeds 124
   Vegetable biryani 64
   Vegetable khichadi 104
   Vegetable moilee 92
   Vegetable samosas 41
pressure cookers 27
puddings *see* desserts
pulao
   Mushroom and chickpea pulao 121
   Pulao rice 120
   Tomato pulao rice 122
pumpkin
   Mixed vegetable Navratan curry 74
   Mulligatawny soup 42
   Pumpkin with panch phoron 73
   Spicy pumpkin 90
   Vegetable chakka 77

Vegetable khichadi 104
Vegetable medley with panch phoron 76

R
radishes
   Vegetable moilee 92
   Watermelon, radish and crunchy rice salad 147
raitas 141
   Boondi raita 151
   Cucumber raita 153
Rajma dal 105
rice 114–15
   Black peppercorn and cumin rice 118
   Lemon rice 117
   Mango rice pudding with palm syrup 181
   Mulligatawny soup 42
   Mushroom and chickpea pulao 121
   Onion uthappams 46
   Pulao rice 120
   Steamed or boiled rice 26
   Tomato pulao rice 122
   Vegetable biryani 64
   Vegetable khichadi 104
ridge gourd 192
Roasted carrot, date and almond salad 150
Rogini sauce 70
roti
   Green mung roti 136
   Missie roti 137

S
saffron 19
   Baked saffron yoghurt pudding with tomato compote 178
   Kum kum tamatar 70
   Mushroom and chickpea pulao 121

Saffron infusion 21
Vegetable biryani 64
Vermicelli pudding 177
salads 140–1
  Kachumber 145
  Mango and pineapple salad 149
  Onion salad 142
  Roasted carrot, date and almond salad 150
  Watermelon, radish and crunchy rice salad 147
Sambar dal 100
samosas, Vegetable 41
semolina 192
  Gujiyas 182
  Orange halwa with sultanas 184
  Upma 56
Sesame chutney 161
shorba 43, 192
Smoky eggplant bhurta 82
snacks 34–5
  Banana chilli and potato pakoras 51
  Beetroot and vegetable 'chops' 55
  Cabbage bondas 49
  Dahi ke kababs 50
  Masala pappadums 37
  Masoor dal wadas 57
  Onion bhajees 59
  Onion uthappams 46
  Pakoras 38
  Vegetable samosas 41
soups
  Mulligatawny soup 42
  Mushroom and coconut shorba 43
spices 16–19
  roasting 19
  spice mixes 20–1
Spicy pumpkin 90
spinach
  Karahi-style baby spinach and mushrooms 88
  Pakoras 38

Spinach kadhi 111
spinach raita 153
Spinach with tofu 78
Vegetable medley with panch phoron 76
Steamed or boiled rice 26
straw potatoes, Crispy 127
street foods
  Bhaturas 133
  Cabbage bondas 49
  Chickpea masala 103
  Pao bhajee 44
  Pooris 132
stuffed vegetables
  Banana chilli and potato pakoras 51
  Grilled Swiss brown mushrooms with spiced breadcrumbs and green peas 53
  Kum kum tamatar 70
  Tomatoes filled with mushrooms and figs 83
sweet potatoes
  Mixed vegetable Navratan curry 74
  Mulligatawny soup 42
  Sweet potato and turnip bhurta 75
  Vegetable chakka 77
  Vegetable khichadi 104
  Vegetable moilee 92
  Vegetable samosas 41

T
tamarind 192
  Eggplant chutney 165
  Sambar dal 100
  Sesame chutney 161
  Spicy pumpkin 90
  Tamarind and ginger chutney 160
  Tamarind pulp 25
tandoor 192
tempering 192

thoran, Green bean 67
tofu 192
  Spinach with tofu 78
tomatoes
  Baked saffron yoghurt pudding with tomato compote 178
  Cauliflower masala 93
  Corn takatak 68
  Jackfruit kolhapuri 91
  Kachumber 145
  Karahi-style baby spinach and mushrooms 88
  Kum kum tamatar 70
  Mulligatawny soup 42
  Okra do pyaz 86
  Pao bhajee 44
  Rajma dal 105
  Smoky eggplant bhurta 82
  Sweet potato and turnip bhurta 75
  Tomato chutney 166
  Tomato pulao rice 122
  Tomatoes filled with mushrooms and figs 83
turmeric 19
turnips
  Mixed vegetable Navratan curry 74
  Mulligatawny soup 42
  Sweet potato and turnip bhurta 75
  Vegetable moilee 92

U
Upma 56
urad dal 192
  Onion uthappams 46
  Pahari dal 110
uthappams, Onion 46

V
Vegetable biryani 64
Vegetable chakka 77

Vegetable khichadi 104
Vegetable medley with panch phoron 76
Vegetable moilee 92
Vegetable samosas 41
Vermicelli pudding 177

W
wadas, Masoor dal 57
Watermelon, radish and crunchy rice salad 147

Y
yoghurt
Baked saffron yoghurt pudding with tomato compote 178
Boondi raita 151
Cucumber raita 153
Dahi chutney 158
Dahi ke kababs 50
Green chutney 161
Spinach kadhi 111

Z
zucchini
Chana dal with coconut and zucchini 109
Vegetable chakka 77
Vegetable medley with panch phoron 76

INDEX

Ragini Dey lives in Adelaide, South Australia, where she runs Ragi's New Deli, a one-stop-shop for her authentic spice blends, pickles and chutneys, cooking classes, and recipe books. From her tiny, one-woman kitchen, she showcases her signature dining concept 'anand bhog', meaning pleasure from pure food.

Ragini shares her home with her husband, son and mother – and her two grandsons on FaceTime!

ACKNOWLEDGEMENTS

It's been a long time since my mother, on requesting a vegan meal on an international flight, was served a gigantic plate of overcooked green beans – no butter, no dressing, not even a smudge of salt or pepper. These days, as a vegan, there is no excuse not to make your tastebuds dance and I am thrilled to have been given the opportunity to embark on this delicious adventure.

Thank you, Fiona, for always believing in me, Simon for making it happen and Nicci for making the humble ingredients (words and vegetables) glow like jewels. Thank you to Jana Liebenstein and Brett Cole for the photos and to Deb Kaloper for styling.

Thank you also to my husband for putting up with the real lack of food while I forsook the kitchen for the desk.

Thank you, most of all, to the readers and the cooks who are inspired to delve into my world of vegan cookery.

Now let the Bhangra begin.

Published in 2025 by Hardie Grant Books, an imprint of Hardie Grant Publishing

Hardie Grant Books (Melbourne)
Wurundjeri Country
Level 11, 36 Wellington Street
Collingwood, Victoria 3066

Hardie Grant North America
2912 Telegraph Ave
Berkeley, California 94705

hardiegrant.com/books

Hardie Grant acknowledges the Traditional Owners of the Country on which we work, the Wurundjeri People of the Kulin Nation and the Gadigal People of the Eora Nation, and recognises their continuing connection to the land, waters and culture. We pay our respects to their Elders past and present.

All rights reserved. No part of this publication may be reproduced, stored in a retrieval system or transmitted in any form by any means, electronic, mechanical, photocopying, recording or otherwise, without the prior written permission of the publishers and copyright holders.

The moral rights of the author have been asserted.

Copyright text © Ragini Dey 2025
Copyright photography © Jana Liebenstein 2025 (recipes) and Brett Cole 2025 (India), except page 203 © Russell Millard 2025
Copyright illustrations © George Saad 2025
Copyright design © Hardie Grant Publishing 2025

 A catalogue record for this book is available from the National Library of Australia

Vegan Indian Food
ISBN 978 1 76145 173 7
ISBN 978 1 76145 174 4 (ebook)

10 9 8 7 6 5 4 3 2 1

Publisher: Simon Davis
Head of Editorial: Jasmin Chua
Project Editor: Nicci Dodanwela
Creative Director: Kristin Thomas
Stylist: Deb Kaloper
Head of Production: Todd Rechner
Production Controller: Jessica Harvie

Colour reproduction by Splitting Image Colour Studio

Printed in China by Leo Paper Products LTD.

 The paper this book is printed on is from FSC®-certified forests and other sources. FSC® promotes environmentally responsible, socially beneficial and economically viable management of the world's forests.

Hardie Grant would like to thank Market Imports, Mud Australia and Made in Japan for the use of props in this book.